Stairways

A True Story of Love, Life, and Death

Steven Zarycki

Editor/Co-scripter: Alexis Paige Zarycki

Co-Editor: Christopher Steven Zarycki

Book Illustration: Codey Vargas

Special Thanks: Nicholas T. Bolt

All Photos Courtesy:

The Zarycki Family

Copyright © 2015 Steven Zarycki

All rights reserved.

ISBN-10: 1512044989
ISBN-13: 978-1512044980

DEDICATION

To my daughter Alexis and to my son Christopher: may the memories of your mother be in your heart till you meet her again.

To both sets of parents: thank you from the bottom of my heart for letting Lori and I experience the love and romance that we had from such an early age, to learn the ups and downs of life, just like a stairway.

To all my friends and family that shared in our life's journey: I am deeply thankful.

To Sue Robbins: without you, I would have never been able to write this book. Because you are the one that introduced me to Lori; and for that I am forever grateful.

To those still fighting the battle against cancer: keep fighting. Don't ever give up. We are here to help.

And to Lori: my soul mate, my lover, my wife, I love you. Thank you for growing up with me, sharing life's adventures with me. For forty years we endured love, passion, romance, pain, and loss. There are no words I can say to bring you back. Until we meet again in paradise, I love you with all of my heart, soul, mind, and body. I love you forever more...Steve.

CONTENTS

FORWARD	i
THE BEGINNING	1-10
SCHOOL YEARS	11-26
LIVING APART: THE SOLUTION	27-32
THE BIG DAY	33-45
STARTING OUR LIFE TOGETHER	46-50
OUR CHILDREN	51-63
THE WORD NOBODY WANTS TO HEAR	64-70
THE ROAD TO RECOVERY	71-75
A SLAP IN THE FACE	76-84
RECOVERY: ROUND TWO	85-97
HOW LONG, DOCTOR?	98-103
THERE IS NO ENDING	104-113
ABOUT THE AUTHOR	114

A Special *Thank You* to the following individuals and places
For being a part of the story of the life of Lori and I:

Northern Highlands Regional High School
Graduate Class of 1980
Allendale, N.J.

The AB&G
Allendale, N.J.

The Alpine Village
Lake George, N.Y.

The Fiesta
Wood-Ridge, N.J.

Allendale Hair Studio
Allendale, N.J.

The Staff at Abramson Cancer Center
Penn Medicine
University of Pennsylvania
Philadelphia, PA

Father Frank DelPrete
of Saint Gabriel's Catholic Church
Saddle River, N.J.

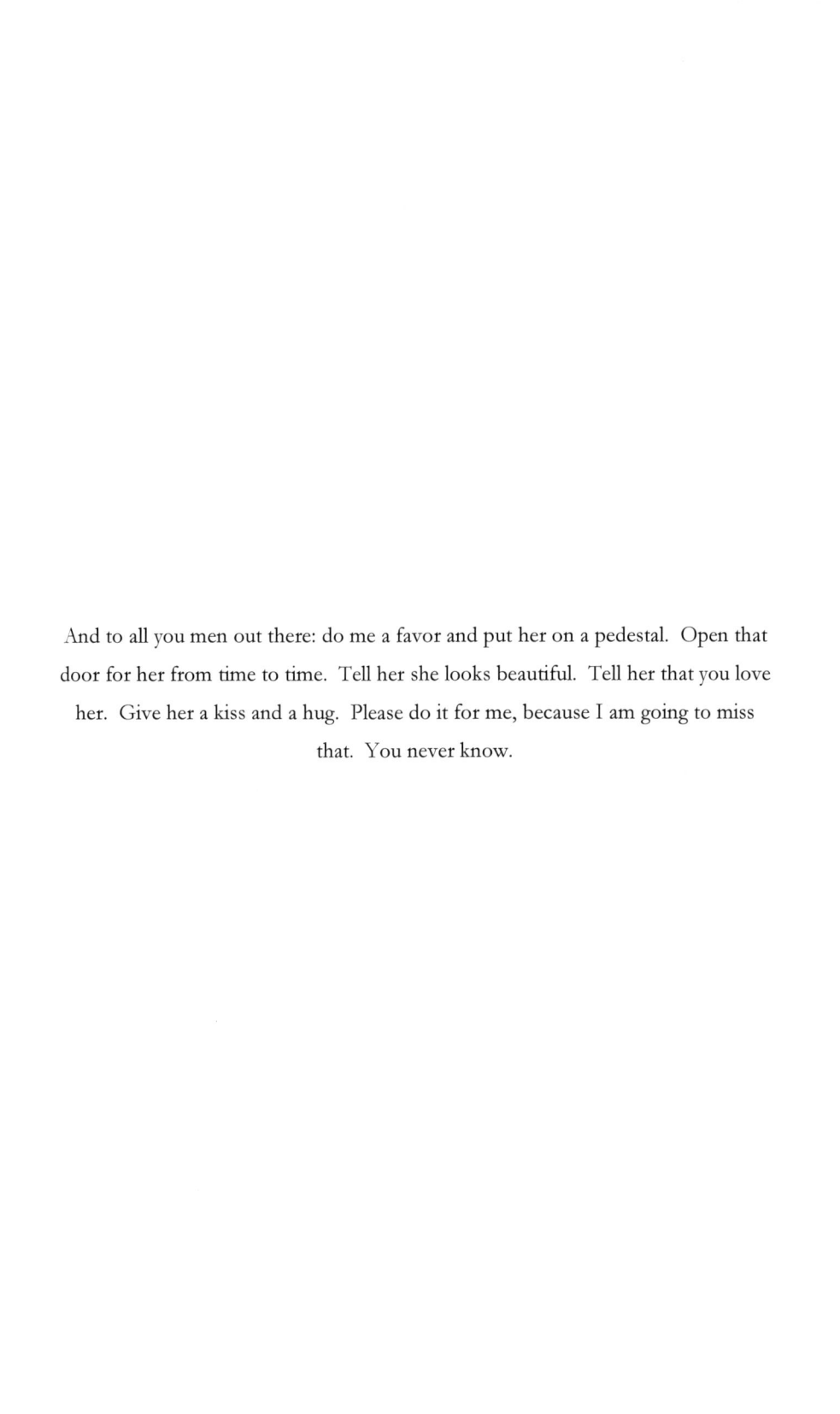

And to all you men out there: do me a favor and put her on a pedestal. Open that door for her from time to time. Tell her she looks beautiful. Tell her that you love her. Give her a kiss and a hug. Please do it for me, because I am going to miss that. You never know.

FORWARD

I told my wife back in 1986 that I could write a book about us. She said to me, "Maybe someday you will." So, she bought me a book with a bunch of blank pages and I started to write. Then for some reason, I put the book to the side after a couple of months of writing…until now.

See, I must tell you this bluntly. I am quite possibly the farthest thing from an experienced writer. I'm just a normal guy that happened to have a very special romance with a very special woman. We fell in love at age fourteen. We were told numerous times we shared a first love together. We were gifted to experience love a second time around. *Old love they called it.* Our romance together was somewhat of a *fairy tale.* One that had no ending, but actually did. I received many calls from friends from the past telling me, "Steve, we wish we had what you and Lori had together through high school and beyond." Social media let me share with friends and family our life's journey as high school sweethearts, as husband and wife, and as a full-time caregiver. We experienced what life had to offer to both of us, and we used our lives to love, learn, and honor each other…till death do us part.

Keep love in your heart always,
Steve

THE BEGINNING

It was my freshman year at Northern Highlands Regional High School in Allendale N.J. I couldn't wait to meet new people, play baseball, and, of course, meet girls. My school was very large; getting to know the layout of the school was challenging. Going up and down stairs, finding classrooms, and my locker were all tasks in and of themselves. As the months went by I began to realize I kept noticing this one girl in the hallways all the time. I noticed she was at my bus stop once or twice, but then learned she was driven to school most of the time by her older brother who was a junior. I didn't know her name, but I was soon to find out who she was. She always smiled at me, and I always smiled back. As we exchanged smiles, I thought to myself, I was going to confront her one day. And then, as fate would have it, I was asked, "Do you want to go to a party?" And this is how our story began.

My friend Sue, whom I've known since eighth grade, asked me this question on a cold morning in January of 1977 at my bus stop; the day before winter recess started. It began to snow very hard that day. The weathermen forecasted that there was a possibility of a foot of snow. I asked Sue, "Who's party is it?" She replied, "It's at Lori's house, but it's her brother's party." I asked Sue, "Who is that?" She replied again, "She's my new girlfriend from school. She moved from Ridgewood to Upper Saddle River in the summer of '76, I met her on the first day of school at our bus stop and we just started talking one day and then became friends." I told Sue that I would go and then she gave me the time. Funny enough, when I asked her where she lived, turns out it was right next door. I was ecstatic. "Wow! The girl next door," I said, with a smile that stretched across my face. "Ok Sue, I'll see you tonight!"

After school I rushed home, got all cleaned up, and told my parents I'm going to a party next door. "I'll see you later!" I yelled, as I left the house. *Wanna to know something funny though?* I found out forty years later that Lori told Sue to ask me to come to the party, but to make me believe that Sue wanted me to go. Later in life, Sue explained to me that Lori felt something was drawing her to me when we were younger, like some sort of internal energy. Something that she couldn't explain. Though at the time it may have sounded strange, I now know what she was talking about. I guess life has a funny sort of way of working itself out like that. *Go figure.*

Anyway, I continued walking a couple of yards down the street to Lori's house and then came to a stop at the top of the hill. Where we lived everywhere was a trek. It must have snowed at least a foot that day, the snow plows were still going back and forth cleaning the streets. I had walked nearly knee-deep in the snow to the back door of her house, on account that nobody had shoveled the driveway. I then rang the doorbell and waited, and waited some more until I finally realized no one was coming to answer the door. I heard loud music playing inside and, being as persistent as I am, I continuously rang the doorbell again…and again…and again until finally an older woman answered the door. At first I thought she was the housekeeper, we did live in an upper scale neighborhood, but I realized it was Lori's grandmother that lived with them.

With a raspy voice, she told me to come in and that everybody was downstairs in the basement. As I began to walk down the basement stairs, I noticed that the beautiful girl who was always staring at me in high school was coming up from the basement. She was about 5 feet and 6 inches tall, mere hundred and some pounds, with blonde hair, and the bluest eyes I've ever seen. I stared, backed up, and then said to her, "Ladies first!" She replied, "That's okay, you come down…Who are you?" Being who I am, I laughed and replied back to her, "Who are you?" She didn't falter and said, "I asked you first!" It was then that I came to the realization that she was playing hard to get. I gave in. "My name is Steve…and yours?" "Lori," she stated. I told her that Sue had invited me over, making sure that was okay. As she smiled, she replied, "Yes, of course," and then continued walking up the stairs.

I can remember every time I passed Sue and Lori in the school hallways Lori was always the first person to say hi to me, then Sue. Yet all I could ever do was say hi back. We always made eye contact and exchanged smiles. I always noticed her. There was always something inside of me was saying, *Steve, just ask her out.* I thought she was gorgeous and that she had a beautiful smile. *So why not ask her out?* What was stopping me? All she could do is say no. I thought to myself; *why not give it a shot?*

    The party was going well. There was food, beer, the music was fun and loud, and there was lots of conversation going on. I was keeping an eye on Lori all night, and I knew she was eyeing me up and down most of the night. She kept coming over to me, asking me if I wanted anything to eat, and I told her I would have something later on. Little did I know, she had a boyfriend *per say* from her old town of Ridgewood present at the party, but I didn't care? By around 10:00 p.m., most of the partygoers were upstairs hanging out. Lori and I were still in the basement talking. She was sitting on top of a freezer with her legs crossed and we were getting *a little acquainted* with each other, if you know what I mean. At times, Lori would sneak in a flirty gesture. She asked me if I had a girlfriend. I told her, "No," and then I asked her if she had a boyfriend. "Not really, just a friend," she replied back to me. That was a *good sign.*

    Lori asked me if I wanted to meet her grandmother. I said, "You mean the older woman that answered the door? Sure, why not!" So we went upstairs, and she started walking up first. As I followed Lori, I noticed she was moving slowly on purpose. So with my two hands, I grabbed her ass and started pushing her up the stairs. She stopped, and spun around to face me. I stopped on the same stair tread as her, and stared into her eyes. And for a second, which seemed like forever, Lori just stopped and smiled at me. I thought I was going to get a slap in the face. Maybe grabbing her ass was too forward? I had to act quickly. I grasped her two hands, held them above her head with my left hand, and with my right arm I placed around her waist. I gazed into her eyes, which were tearing up with joy and happiness. I drew her close to me and *kissed her.* After that first kiss, I released her arms and they fell slowly around my neck. She gave me another kiss, and said, "You're the one." I didn't even bother to ask her what that meant, but I kept it close to me. It meant something to me, but I wouldn't find out what it meant until years later. We kept kissing each other on the stairs and holding each other. We were bound to be together. We eventually made our way back down the stairs, where I proceeded to pick her up and sit her back down on the freezer. We kept on kissing some more. I think after that point it was quite obvious that Lori and I had something going on, but the *'friend'* she had there at the party was still a problem.

Later on in the night, Lori, her *'friend'*, and I somehow ended up in her bedroom talking. The *'friend'* was very agitated at her and began yelling at her. I didn't take to well to his trash mouth. So, I punched him and with little to no hesitation, pushed him against her poster bed and broke it. I remember the look on Lori's face. She was so mad at him, practically livid. She sternly told him to leave her house and not to ever come back. I guess *I won* that fight, and let me tell you the prize was beautiful!

I asked her to go out with me that very night after all the craziness died down, and she gave the swiftest yes I ever received. Actually, it was the first one I ever received from a girl. "Something feels funny," she said. "Me?" I asked. "No, like we were together before, like I told you in the basement," she stated. I paid no attention to whatever she was saying because I was too infatuated with her. I was fourteen and now had a beautiful girlfriend and frankly that was all that mattered to me at that moment in time. But, as I've come to realize with age, there really was something else inside me that kept telling me that wasn't all that mattered. There was something more; something deeper.

The time was now around 11:30pm, but after kissing Lori for a while, it had to be at least another hour or two later. Lori and I finally walked out of her bedroom, hand in hand, into the family room. A few people were still left from the party, all just sitting in the family room. When they looked at us and said, "What's this?", we didn't explain ourselves to them. "It is what it is" we articulated to them, and kept the rest of our new romance to ourselves. As I was about to leave, I told Lori to give me a call and gave her my number while walking out the door. No sooner than having left the party, I came home to my room with the phone ringing. It was Lori. "I miss you!" she exclaimed. "I just left there!" I said to her. "I know. Are you coming over in the morning?" "Sure," I told her in a firm tone. "Okay," she said. Wrapping up the conversation, I said good night and, of all things, she replied to me "Good night, my prince," in a soft spoken voice. I must admit, I was bit surprised at that comment. No one had ever said that to me before. But Lori, as I was finding, was full of surprises; and I was starting to enjoy it.

As I lay in bed that night, I felt a sort of *déjà vu* with me and Lori, but I couldn't put my finger on it. I really started to have deep thoughts about what she said when we first met; something about knowing me from somewhere else. I had a dream that night, one I will never forget. It was about a carriage ride with her, but it didn't go anything farther than that. It was us going for a carriage ride in a park, her and I, and then I woke up. *Weird.*

The next morning, I went to Lori's house around 9:00 a.m. Her parents weren't home because they were on a cruise. Like a gentleman, I helped clean up all the garbage that was scattered around the house from the party the night before. Somebody got sick in the bathroom that night and locked the door. So Lori's grandmother and I, whom I learned was named Johanna, pried open the door. After helping Johanna out, I found Lori in her bedroom straightening up. She gave me a kiss and began to tell me that her Uncle Bob paid a visit to the party last night. Someone was definitely going to get into a little trouble when her parents came back.

As I sat talking with her, I slowly learned about Lori and her family. Lori had a really kind and caring family. She had an older brother, Tommy, and a younger sister, Kathi. Lori was the middle child out of the three. Her parents, Jo Ann and Tony, owned a paving and construction company in Ridgewood. Her mother's father, Grandpa Joe, started the business back in 1942. There was a lot to learn about the family, and luckily I had all the time to do so.

Lori and I hung out most of that day. She was even nice enough to make me lunch. At about mid-day, the doorbell rang. It was Lori's friends Sue and Ann, along with their boyfriends. We all hung out for a while, listening to some 8-track tapes in Lori's room. Lori was looking at me the entire time. She had this disgusted and annoyed expression on her face. I think it was blatantly obvious that she wanted them to leave so her and I could be alone. Then, all of a sudden, the two couples started making out. Lori and I didn't. For one reason or another, we didn't want to display ourselves, we were private in that way. So we just talked, and in about forty-five minutes later, her friends left.

Now it was our time to be alone. We embraced each other on the bed, and then on the floor. She came down on top of me on all fours. She gave me little kisses all around. She was being playful, and it was turning me on. I spun her around and brought her to the floor and started teasing back. I let go of her arms.

She put them around me and gave me a playful whisper, "I love you." I countered the remark and I said to her, "I love you, too!" I know we just met each other, how could we be in love? But hey, we were fourteen. We had fun that day, so much fun that we actually fell asleep together on the couch. It was an amazing feeling. She asked me if I wanted to stay for dinner. "Of course" I said, but I had to make sure that my mother was okay with it though.

    Thankfully my mother was, and Lori made me my first dinner: steak, with potatoes and salad. It was delicious. She won my heart that day: cooking and all. After the meal was done, like any gent, I gave Lori a kiss goodnight and walked home. Then, like clockwork, I walked in my door and the phone rang. It was Lori again. I swear she must have either watched me while I walked down the street or had the timing down of how long it took me to get back to my house from hers. "What?" I said. "I miss you," Lori replied in a sad voice. "Do you want to go to the movies tomorrow?" I asked. "Yes!" Lori replied. I said good night again and hung up the phone. Most guys would have thought it was a bit crazy, how fast we were moving, but boy I'm telling you I could already hear the bells.

    Our first date was the movies. My father and mother were able to meet Lori for the first time. I walked to Lori's house to pick her up, and then we walked together back to mine. Obviously, we were too young to drive so we had to get the parents to drive us. She came into the house to meet my dad, Walter, and my two younger brothers, Tommy and Peter. Then she met my mother, Jean. My mother didn't seem interested in Lori and what she had to say. It made me think that no matter what girl or woman you bring home to meet your mother, they're never good enough for their son.

    My father was the one that took us to the late showing at the movie theater in Ramsey. The movie playing that night was *Saturday Night Fever*, it was the start of the disco era. I could relate to the movie somewhat, being it was filmed in Brooklyn where most of my cousins lived at the time. I had the same exact shoes that were in the movie as well. Those were the days of silk shirts, bell-bottom pants, and terrible rooster hair styles. The movie was great, what we saw of it that is. Our lips were together most of the time. At the completion of the movie, my father took us home. I'm not going to lie, not driving really sucked. We had to rely on our parents to drive us around everywhere. It seemed as if it was nearly impossible for us to really be *alone* together. Though we found our ways.

A few days later her parents came back from the cruise and, wouldn't you guess it, they found out about the party. Lori and her brother, Tommy, were grounded for a week. That week was a lonely one for me: I wasn't able to hang out at her house or meet her parents till the next week. The only way I could spend time with Lori was during school or by talking to her on the phone. We would pass notes in between classes: at that time period it was our form of today's *texting*.

Finally, the day came when Lori's punishment was over and I was able to meet her parents. I walked up the front yard stairway and rang the doorbell. Lori answered the door, gave me a hug and kiss but I could tell that she was a bit nervous. I told her I would be on my best behavior. She brought me inside to meet her father, who was sitting in front of the television in his lounger. She said, "Dad, this is Steven." "Hello, Sir!" I said confidently, while shaking his hand firmly as he sat comfortably in his chair. Word of advice, have a firm handshake when meeting a girl's father. Lori then brought me to meet her mother. She guided me in to the back room where her mother was ironing. "Mom," she said, "This is Steven." "Hello, Mrs. B. You look lovely today." That was it; I was in with the parents. I already met her brother and sister, so now the only thing left was to formally meet the grandmother of the household, Johanna. Even though I semi-helped her with the dirty bathroom the morning after the party, the first day Lori and I met, I didn't actually have a conversation with her or even really say hi. As it came to be, I found out that she loved Elvis Presley like a son, cooked meals like Julia Childs, and smoked cigarettes like a chimney. She was the person that taught Lori how cook, someone that Lori deeply loved. Needless to say, I knew I had to be nice to her and the rest of the family, so that's exactly what I did.

As the days of us together went on, Lori and I were gradually getting cabin fever. We couldn't drive, so we were forced to make our own adventures. One time, we walked to the public bus stop, hopped on the first bus that came, and went to New York City. *Were we nuts?* I didn't think so, but if our parents found out we would have been dead. However, I wouldn't have traded anything for the fun times we had. We were having the time of our lives being two kids in love.

We walked around 42nd Street, Times Square, Central Park, had some pizza for lunch and then hopped on the bus again to go back home. About a mile from the house, her mother passed by us in the car. She stopped and picked us up. She asked us, "Where are you two coming from?" Lori said, "The mall." Lori was always a quick thinker.

Later that day, after I had went home, she called me a few hours later. "What's up?" I said, "That was close sweetie; we have to be more careful. I'll see you tomorrow in school. I love you." And then there was a pause. Without any hesitation, Lori asks, "Aren't you going to say it?" "Yes," I said, "I love you too," and hung up the phone. Something was definitely going on then. I didn't know what it was, but I believed it would be life-changing. I couldn't explain how I felt; it was like butterflies in my stomach circling round and round. I wanted to say something to Lori but I didn't know how to. Was it possible that we were falling in love, but at such a young age? Could this be the girl I am supposed to spend the rest of my life with? I had no clue.

Freshman year was flying by fast. I was always walking Lori to her classes first, and then running like hell to my classes. When the bell rang for students to change classes, I would run to her, take her books, and walk her to another class. I was always there for Lori. Back and forth…back and forth. This was a daily routine for us. At the end of the day, I was exhausted, but Lori admired it. We always kissed, and passed a notes back and forth whenever we saw each other. It's too bad we didn't have lunch at the same time; then again I probably wouldn't have been able to focus and eat. See, her last name started with a "B", so her lunch period was first, whereas my last name began with a "Z", so I had it second. After school, the rest of my day would consist of either baseball practice or a game. However, Lori would wait for me, and then we would then take the late bus home together. We would attempt to work on our homework, but always ended up making out, either at my house or hers. But most of the time, I was over her house because I enjoyed my time there. Her family was welcoming and always enjoyed my company.

In the middle of May we had a day off from school, for some reason I cannot remember, and Lori and I made up this saying, if you want to call it that. "You wanna?" was the term. It meant intercourse and Lori and I never had it before. The two of us were romantic, even at age fourteen. We had our special moment. That was our alone time, as we called it. Holding hands at school and a little kiss here and there was common, but we really didn't like to showcase or display our emotions to the world. Imagine that coming from fourteen year old kids. On this day in May nobody was home at Lori's house. We assumed that everybody was out doing something. I ultimately gained the courage to say to her, "You wanna?" And you know what, words cannot express how I felt when I said that. I wanted her, and only her. I could sense that we were both scared that someone might come home, so we opened the window to be able to hear outside if any cars were coming down the driveway.

This was a first for both of us. She wanted it to be special and so did I. She wanted to feel that I loved her. She wanted to feel it first from me. I didn't want it to be that quick, meaningless type of love either. It would come from my heart and soul. The way we made love surprised me; it was like we had performed it before together, but in a different time. We spent over two hours or so in bed; it came naturally to us. It was such a romantic encounter for two young teenagers; you wouldn't expect it at all. After our encounter, she put on her bathrobe, and I dressed myself. She walked me to the door, and I gave her a kiss goodbye. The words *I love you* came out of my mouth first, and then from hers. I couldn't think straight walking home. My mouth was shut. I was in deep thought. *What just happened to us? What just happened to me?* I was in love, and I never felt this feeling before. Yes, there were a couple more encounters after that with Lori, and every time felt as if it was the first time. We always said that we saw fireworks in each other afterwards. We laughed about it. *Were we really in love so early in life? Is this normal?* I was sure that is was normal, and it felt absolutely beautiful.

Freshmen year was ending. Lori told me she had the amazing opportunity to travel to Sicily with her cousin Paula and her husband John. I was at a loss for words. *How could she leave me behind like that?* I said to her, "But…what about me?" "What about you?" Lori replied. "Do what you want, I'm done!" I exclaimed with anger and sadness. At that moment, I broke up with Lori. She cried, and I was heartbroken. I was stupid. But what do you say when the girl you love is leaving to another country? I guess when you're fourteen you don't really know what *to* say.

Summertime was here and Lori was gone. My parents had rented a house on Long Beach Island, which is an island located on the Jersey Shore, for the family to enjoy. While at the beach, I met some acquaintances in Lori's absence; even had a fling or two. But, not a day went by when I didn't think of her; *my first love*. Two of the hottest bands that summer, Boston and Meatloaf, were always on the radio. Some of their songs reminded me of Lori. I felt so alone. Playing this music on the beach didn't help me at all coping with the loss of Lori. I had lost my best-friend. I felt misplaced not being able to see her or spend time with her.

And then, like that, the summertime came...and went. Yet the only thing I seemed to take away from that summer was a dark tan. I was really looking forward to seeing Lori again at the start of the school year. But, I wondered, would she feel the same?

SCHOOL YEARS

Time for school to start again. It was our sophomore year, 1977-1978. Still not old enough to drive, but soon I will be. Here we go again, another year. I was walking down the hall of the school and saw Lori talking to her girlfriend Sue. Wow! Lori looked great! It was two months since I last saw her. I slowly walked up behind her, like a cat ready to pounce at its prey, and gave her a bear hug and a gentle kiss on the cheek. She turned around quickly and I thought I was going to get a slap in the face again, but I didn't. I received a long, cold stare from her. She sized me up from head to toe. "Hello, how was your summer?" she said. With hesitation I replied, "Well, a black cloud hung over me the entire summer. I didn't really enjoy it. I was all by myself most of the time. I was alone." I looked at her with guilt and sadness. It seemed as though a tear was building up in her right eye as I turned and left to go to class alone.

I found out later in the day that Lori had a long distance relationship with a boy she met in Sicily. He was her cousin's husband's younger brother. His name was Joe. Forty years later, I found that this was not true. Lori made this all up to make me jealous, and it worked. Joe *was* John's younger brother, two years younger than Lori, but he was told to guard her during the entire trip to Sicily. I didn't know this, but apparently American women were considered easy prey during that time. Years later, I still laugh and cry about this. Lori truly did love me, she just liked to play games and tease me from time to time and I thank her for that. It made her who she was. Anyways, the school year was going by very fast. Lori was not dating anybody at the time. I had a girlfriend. Lori hated seeing her with me. She was very jealous; she hardly talked to me. She and I ultimately didn't last, and we parted ways sometime in the middle of sophomore year.

It was April now. I was getting dressed for a baseball game. I was pitching that day; I was very anxious to pitch against this team, but extremely nervous. I started walking to the field, profusely sweating, when I saw Lori sitting on the bleachers. This was pretty strange to me; I hardly saw her the entire school year and she shows up to this particular game? I walked over to her and said "Hi." She smiled, wished me good luck, and blew me a kiss. All my nervousness went away, and I thanked her for it. I pitched a great game that day because of her. Knowing she was there watching me and all. And then, as I walked to the back of the dugout, I thought to myself: I should have just stopped, grabbed her, told her I was sorry and that I loved her and what a fool I was. I still had a lot of feelings for her, and I kept thinking that we were meant to be together. I can't let her go I thought. I need to win her back. I loved her, and deep down inside there was the burning desire to be with her. I knew that she loved me, her friends all told me so. Lori only wanted me in her life and no one else. Nothing was going to stop me.

Lori must have known when I pitched in my baseball games because she came to all of them. I found out that Lori used to answer the phones for the coaches instead of participating in gym class. She would always ask the coaches about my pitching rotations. *Smart girl.* I must have been blind not to ever notice. She was always one step ahead of me. She loved to watch me play baseball. I would sometimes hit a batter because he was crowding the plate or brush him back a little. During the game, Lori would say, "You hit that batter!" And jokingly, I would say, "He was looking at you though!" Lori would get very impressed at that, and blew me a kiss every time. The coaches would get pissed when I yelled to Lori. They thought I wasn't paying attention and would tell me to run back to the dugout. I guess Lori just had that effect on me.

The school had year ended, and I said goodbye to my sophomore year. Summer time was here again, yet now I could drive. It was a blessing that I didn't have to ask for rides anymore. Lori, unfortunately, was not home for most of the summer again. This made me really upset…again. This time she went to Connecticut and Florida with her family. However she was always sending me letters through the mail each day. She said in one of her letters that her parents were afraid she would take a bus home to come see me; so they watched her closely during her stay in Florida. She kept saying she was miserable without me there. I kept telling her it would be okay. Funny enough, I kept every letter she wrote me that summer. She wrote things about her love for me, her dreams of living in a house on the water down on the Jersey Shore, long walks with me on the beach, and even spending the rest of her life with me. As I would sit and read and re-read these letters I couldn't stop thinking to myself: *why did I ever break up with this girl at the end of freshmen year? Was I an idiot or something?* I definitely was not thinking. I must have been very selfish to even fathom the idea of breaking away from this girl who loved me so much. I knew that I wanted her back, so I had to prove it to her. I had to prove to her that I truly loved her as much as she loved me, and nobody else. From then on, I would make sacrifices for her. Whatever it took, anything to get her back.

It was now junior year, 1978-1979. I was walking down the stairway from the second floor between classes and I ran into Lori, who was coming up the stairway from the first floor, almost like the first time we met. She was wearing heels, a plaid skirt, and a blouse that had lace around the neck. A little overdressed, I thought, but Lori loved her clothes and she did work in a retail store. Lori was also learning how to model at a modeling school. One day, she stopped me and asked if I could check the tires on her car after school. She bought a used, red Camaro with her own money. I was a little jealous at first, but I said "yes" without hesitation. This was the chance I had been waiting for with Lori. *I will not screw this up.*

Lori had gotten out of school early because she had a work assignment, which was part of her school credits. She waited for an hour for me. On her own accord, she called in sick that day. I always wondered why. I went over to her car and checked her tires. They all seemed fine. I noticed that they were brand new, so I was confused why she would ask me to check brand new tires. *What is going on here?* Lori then asked me if I could drive her home. With happiness in my voice I said, "Sure, of course I will!" I opened the car door for her, and we were off. I decided to take the long way home. I began the conversation and asked her what she had been up to lately, if she had a boyfriend, how her friends were. You know, the usual conversation pieces that you try to use to pry information out of someone that you are very interested in. She said, "Obviously nothing, and no, I don't have a boyfriend at the moment." This was my chance to spill everything to her on how I felt. I began to tell her how both summers were terrible for me. I told her I thought of her every chance I could, and that I missed her every minute, every second, and every hour she wasn't with me. After saying what I had to get off my chest, Lori then told me she was angry and confused at me for the entire time we parted ways. She mentioned that she would give me a second chance, and I decided to ask, "Would you give me a second chance?" "Of course I will, my sweetheart," she said with a huge smile on her face. "And should I give you a second chance Lori?" I asked. "You better!" she said.

We made it safely to my house and I stepped out of the car first to open Lori's passenger door. As Lori stepped out with the engine still running, we walked next to each other and stopped in front of the car. "What are you doing later?" I asked. "Not much, do you want to do something?" Lori replied. "Movies?" I inquired. "Sure," she said. I gave her a little kiss; she got back in her car, looked at me with a smile, and drove off down our street to her house.

I didn't have a car yet, but I had my license. So, Lori picked me up at 9pm from my house. She came to the front door, we went inside, said hello to my family, and then were off again. We went to the Ramsey Movie Theater, like old times. I bought her soda and popcorn; she loved Coca-Cola and that was all she really drank. The movie playing at that time was a comedy. It was kind of boring to be frank and I was becoming restless and tense, and so was Lori. I put my arm around her, her head slowly dipped down to my shoulder. "You ok?" I asked. "It's perfect," she said. I moved my head slowly towards her lips. She looked up at me with the light reflecting off her eyes from the movie screen. It seemed like she had tears in her eyes; not for the movie, but for me. Slowly, I kissed her, her arms embracing my shoulders as if she wasn't ever going to let me go and I said for the second time in my life to her, "I love you," and she squeezed me tighter. Now with actual tears in her eyes, she said, "I love you too, Steven". Our sparks, and emotions, rekindled in that one moment. "Don't ever leave me again," she said. "I won't, I promise," I said. We left the theater early. I started the car and drove off.

As we were driving around, I took a deep breath and said to Lori, "I am sorry for the pain I caused." She replied, "Steven, I am too." She then slowly put her body on my lap while I was driving, stretching her legs across the passenger seat, putting her arms around my neck, placing her head on my shoulder. We then began kissing while I was driving which, now that I think about it, was probably not the smartest idea at the time. But we were young daredevils and we took our chances. At that moment, the words just came out of my mouth. "Lori, you wanna?" "Yes, Steven, so much. With you, and only you, for the rest of my life." So I put my quick thinking to  work, and I found a cheap hotel not far from our homes. We didn't care what kind of place it was, it was the fact we had our time together. That's what we cared about. It was a special night for the both of us. We made up for all the lost time when we had been apart. Even though we'd only been apart for a short period of time, it still seemed like a lifetime. We knew that we were meant for each other. That's when we made a pact to each other to not to let anybody or anything get between us and our love ever again. That following Monday we were back at school, together as one and stronger than ever. Some people were shocked, and others knew it was meant to be. We kept up with our daily routines: work, school, baseball, singing lessons, modeling. We were both very busy individuals, but we made sure we had time for ourselves.

It was the summer of '79 now, and it was fantastic. We had barbecues at our parent's houses, took walks on the beach, and went everywhere and anywhere. I met most of Lori's aunts, uncles, and cousins, and she did the same with mine. That summer, I finally received a car from my parents. It was a great blessing. It was a 1974 T-Bird. It was the size of a boat and a gas guzzler, but I couldn't complain because it was free. We drove more and more now that I had a car. Lori was now working at a shoe store and I was working in a clothing store not too far away. You couldn't tell us that we weren't dressed right for the times. We had the most fashionable wardrobes that summer and coming senior year, due to our discounts. However, we still saved a lot of money. I would also contribute to Lori's 'hope chest,' which was what she called the savings fund for if she would ever become married.

After work, Lori would pick me up or I would pick her up, and we would go out to eat, hang out, talk; it all depended on how our mood was. One day Lori and I were talking at lunch and we brought up the past and what kind of mistakes we had made. We looked at it as a learning experience for both of us. We also talked about the upcoming year; it would be our best year together because we were going to be seniors in high school. We talked about things all kids growing up do: what path we were going to take after we graduate, where we going to be. It was a mystery for both of us, one we were both trying to solve. I think the main thing we were both worried about at that time was what was going to happen to us after our senior year. But it was still summer, and we didn't want to spoil it.

Lori and I still had to abide by our parents' rules because we still lived at home. So if we went away for the weekend, we had to let them know where we were going. My car unfortunately died that summer and it was going to cost me a lot to fix it. So, I decided to sell it as-is and went out and bought a new car with the money I saved from working; a 1978 Chevrolet Monte Carlo. That was my second baby, and Lori loved it. This car had no center console, which was great because if Lori was tired, she would lie down across the front seat and her head rested in my lap. Times were good back then; just her and I, riding in my Chevrolet.

We went to the Jersey Shore on the weekends. It was great because it wasn't far at all. We would stay the night at a hotel, take long walks on the beach, and talk about the future. We did that a lot actually. Lori took me one day to her favorite hair salon, Allendale Hair Studio. She told her hair stylist, Roberta, to make my hair wavier. I had no clue what that meant. She gave me a sensor perm; it wasn't too bad. All that mattered was if Lori liked it. I just had to get used to it, because I always parted my hair down the middle. Lori also wanted to pierce my ear. I let her attempt to try to do it for me. Lori began numbing my ear lobe with an ice cube and when I saw the needle coming close I freaked out. That was it. No more experimenting on Steven. Overall, from doing this and that, Lori and I always kept busy. It was a constant learning experience for both of us.

Lori always loved talking about her dreams, and what she dreamed about for the both of us. It was all so perfect for Lori and me. But, we also had are down days; we are human after all. Life wasn't always so peachy. Like any normal couple, we argued. Sometimes about little things, and sometimes it ended in us not even seeing each other for a day or two, but that was how we grew. I was always the *initiator* of our relationship, and Lori enjoyed that. She adored that I was romantic, passionate, and gentle when we made love. She was always in a relaxed, dream state when she was with me. One day, I was joking around and I said to her that I could write a book about us which would describe in detail some of our adventures and encounters. Lori said, "Maybe someday you will, and when you do, I want the first book and I want you to sign it for me." I told her, "Of course."

It was now senior year. It was our turn now. We were officially high school seniors; the year we thought our shit didn't stink. We took turns driving each other to school, but most of the time she and I worked so much that we had to take separate cars. Lori and I kept writing notes and letters to each other between classes. A lot of the letters were poems that she would dream up for me, other times the letters would be about small talk or arguments. Either way, I loved them. One day, she gave me a letter saying how she wanted to spend the rest of her life with me. The letter was so detailed; she said she wanted to have a house on the water, with two kids. Pretty much the perfect family. At the end of that specific letter, she signed it as 'Love, Lori Z'. I had to stop and think for a second after that letter. *Was I going to ask her to marry me and spend the rest of my life with her? What if I didn't want to get married yet?* Life seemed like it was moving way too fast with Lori, and I was only eighteen.

The next couple of days after reading that letter, I was miserable. I knew that my life was changing every day. I tried not to show it in front of Lori, but she was smart. She sensed that something was wrong with me. I was looking for colleges with Division 1 baseball teams hoping I would catch a break and get some type of scholarship. But sadly, it wasn't meant to be. Even though I made varsity freshman year, I decided not to play baseball my senior year and my coaches were extremely pissed at me. They knew I had a good shot at pitching for Florida State

University, but I basically threw my chances away. I was struggling. I didn't know what to do. There was a growing rift within my heart and soul between the love I had for Lori and the possibility of losing her. She told me a couple of times, when I asked her for her advice on this, that our relationship would be ok. But I knew that deep down inside of her she didn't want me to go to college. I could always hear it in her voice; she was holding back tears. If I left her, the days and months apart from each other would tear us up.

Eventually, I had to make the biggest decision of my life. I confronted my parents and I told them I wasn't going to college. They were not happy. My parents didn't understand how much I loved Lori. Disoriented, I left my house and took a drive. I thought about a lot of things on that drive. Here I am, eighteen years old, throwing away college, a chance at pitching for a great college baseball team and possibly making it to the Big Leagues. I was going to graduate in a couple of months from high school. *What was I to do?* I'm in love with Lori, and she is in love with me. *But what do I do?*

At that instant, I swung the wheel of the car, turned around, and went straight to her house. I rang the doorbell, and she answered it. I told her to come outside and I needed to talk. She looked nervous; possibly thinking I didn't want to see her anymore. With tears in my eyes, I said to her, "Lori, I'm not going to college. I want to go out in the working world. I love you, and want to spend the rest of my life with you." I think after I said that she almost fainted at that moment. People probably thought I was nuts for doing that, they may still think so, but I don't care and never will. She gave me the biggest hug and kiss after that. I knew she was glad, but for a while she kept saying it was her fault I didn't go further with school. I kept telling her that it wasn't her fault; it never was. It was my own decision, and that was it. Lori decided she wasn't going to college either and I was fine with that as well. Actually, to be frank, I was very happy. Some weeks passed, and by my parents eventually came to terms with me not attending college. They were still worried about me, like any parents would be, but Lori and I were working hard, saving money, and spending some of it on important items for the future.

Lori and I made sure we did all the traditions right, whether it was attending family gatherings or relative's birthdays; we were always there. Family and friends knew that we were the perfect couple, and that we truly shared a bond in love that nobody could break. Both our parents went out together a couple of times. Lori and I knew they would converse about us, mostly about good things. However, the most popular topic was what the future held for us as a couple, and as individuals. Lori and I made our own decisions about our future, and nobody else could interfere with them.

Senior year was going great for us. Both of us spent every day together. We went for long car rides, we went to parties, and we did a lot together. However, Lori and I kept to ourselves a lot. We had our close friends and all, but it was mainly us two always spending time together; that's all we wanted. I asked Lori, "Don't you want to spend time with your friends?" She said, "I do at school." And then she asked me, "What about you?" I said the same exact same thing to her. I guess that, deep down inside, we never wanted to be apart from each other.

As the year went on, we still continued to spend all the time we could together. One time Lori had asked me to help her babysit the neighbor's kids. She was watching a toddler and an infant. I winged it as best as I could to help Lori out. I didn't have kids at the time, but I used common sense and tried my best at being a mock father. Lori showed me how to make a bottle for the infant, change a diaper, and burp the baby the correct way. Maybe this experience was preparing me for later on in life when I had my own kids?

We tried to change things up from time to time instead of driving around in a car or hanging out at the house or in town. One day we decided to try our hand at sports. Lori wasn't really the athletic type. The only sport or activity she was involved in was skiing. I actually taught her how to ski. I had been skiing since I was ten years old. One day up on the mountain, Lori caught an edge on her ski and fell into me, lodging her ski pole inside my mouth. That's all it took, and she never went skiing again. She didn't want to 'hurt me' was always her excuse for not to ski again. Then as we got older it was 'it's too cold.' She preferred using a motorized machine, like a snowmobile. I could never catch her! One sporting event we loved to go to together was hockey games. Oh, how we loved hockey. She would love to go just to watch the players fight. The game of hockey is fast-paced and Lori enjoyed that. But, if I was to take her to a boxing match, she would say it was barbaric. *I could never figure that one out.* We also liked to go bowling together. Nonetheless, if Lori broke a nail, the game was over. We went camping a lot too, though Lori wasn't the most rustic woman. I made sure the tent had no bugs and that bathrooms were close by. Otherwise, I caught hell. We also did a lot of hiking. This took us to some amazing views. Viewing historic sites and taking pictures was another one of our favorite things; my hobby was photography. I loved taking pictures of Lori; she was my best subject. I tried to do a lot of things Lori wanted to do; or eventually she made me do it with her. One of the activities she dragged me to do was horseback riding. I soon discovered Lori was an excellent equestrian. She rode English and Western style. I rode backwards; at least it seemed like I did. It was an uncomfortable experience for me, but nonetheless, we enjoyed it together; and we did it again many times over.

When it was time for prom season, Lori wanted to go out and get a dress. I took her to the mall so she can shop around and find one. She found a beautiful blue-colored layered dress. This meant that I had to find a tuxedo in blue. There wasn't a store in town that had one. After searching diligently, and calling numerous stores miles and miles away from town, I eventually found one. It was located in New York State, just over the border from our town. We had two weeks before the prom, and one night, Lori and I were on the phone and I was just joking around and I said, "You want to go to bed tonight?" She said, "What!?" "Not that way," I laughed. "Let's leave the phones off the hook and place them next to us on the pillow. So when you fall asleep, I can listen to you breathe." She paused for a minute and said, "How romantic! What a sweet thing to do." So we did it, and in the morning, I whistled into the phone. She heard the sound and picked up the phone, saying, "Good morning, honey." I said, "Good morning, my wife." She was shocked. She said, "What did you say?" "You heard what I said," I replied back. I think that statement made her day, and the rest of her life. She said, "Steve, I love you till the day I die. What you said will come true." "What, the wife part?" I said. "Yes!" Lori exclaimed back. "Well, I wouldn't have said it if I didn't mean it." I told her. "I'll pick you up in half hour," I said. It sounded like she was crying when she hung up the phone. I went to the local store before I picked her up. I bought her a coffee and a little bouquet of flowers and then I went to her house. She came out the back door as usual; and there I was leaning against the car with my simple gifts of affection. She ran down the stairs, almost stumbling over her feet. She gave me the biggest kiss and hug and said, "I wish every morning could be like this with you." I said, "If you wish hard enough, it may just happen."

Well, it's now prom night. I went to Lori's house and rang the doorbell; she looked beautiful when she answered the door. I gave her flowers for her wrist, and she gave me a corsage for my jacket. Her mom started taking pictures of us. Then, I took her over to my house, and my mother took her pictures of us as well. We then left for the prom.

Lori was very quiet around people. She was what you would call a 'people watcher.' She would sit back and watch everything that was going on. I usually was the one that socialized. So Lori followed my lead, and she was at my side as we entered the prom, keeping an open mind about how it was going to turn out. As we entered, we could see that all our friends were there in their own section. We talked with most of them but still kept in our bubble. You could tell that some people were drunk; I mean, it was prom. Lori and I enjoyed everything. We danced, tried the food, danced some more, and then said our goodbyes leaving the prom before it was finished. We headed right to the beach and fell asleep. Never again would I sleep on a beach; there were too many gnats and insects eating us alive. In the morning, we went to a cheap hotel. It was a long weekend for bonding. We did a lot talking, per usual, and enjoyed the sun and the beautiful weather. But most of all, we had fun together. We were together, just Lori and I.

A week later, we were graduating from high school. My parents and her parents sat together with other relatives during the graduation. The ceremony that evening was extremely long. Speech after speech. Best wishes and good lucks. We threw our caps in the air at the final congratulation. Lori and I made it. We finally graduated. I was very proud of myself and proud of Lori. We said our goodbyes to our friends, and told them we would see them at future reunions and possible get-togethers. Our friends wished us good luck in our future endeavors; we were on our way.

After graduation, we went out to dinner with our parents that night at a local eatery called the AB&G, located in Allendale, NJ. It was just down the street from the high school in the center of town. Lori and I used to stop there after school and grab a burger before we went home. It was a nice place to relax and enjoy our new found freedom. Lori's grandfathers actually use to go there back in the early 60's. The food was excellent. Still is. We thanked both sets of parents for dinner that night and all that they had done for us.

    Looking back at our years in high school, Lori and I learned a lot from each other. We weren't perfect, but we tried to be. We learned to be honest with each other, how to be grown-ups, and how to respect each other's opinions. We always talked about our problems and resolved them. We were living in our own world, a world that we created. We were about to embark on a new journey, one we were planning on taking together.

We decided to go away for a couple of days after graduation to unwind. We wondered where we could travel to be isolated from everyone, or almost everyone. We packed for three days and headed north to the Adirondack region of upstate New York. Lori and I had heard of a town called Lake George, so we headed there. It was a tourist town; there were a lot of different activities to partake in, such as parasailing or hiking. There were a ton of people around too, and we didn't want to stay in a hotel in town. We wanted something more rustic and secluded, like a cabin in the woods. I drove out into the outskirts of town along Route 9, about a mile out, and there it was, The Alpine Village. It was as though it was meant just for us, waiting for our arrival. The village compound had a main lodge on the lake, and cabins spread out in the woods. The cabins all had fireplaces as well. It was a tranquil place in the pines along the lake. Lori and I had open minds. We always made the best out of nothing. We checked in and they gave us our cabin. Number 9. *How ironic.* The number 9 was my baseball jersey number all throughout high school. Lori said that it must be our lucky cabin. I told her how lucky I was to have her. I received a kiss for that.

Unfortunately, our cabin was on a hill so we had to climb stairs. A lot of them. I jokingly mentioned all our encounters with stairways to Lori, and she said, "That's no joke!" I replied, "I was only kidding." We opened the door and we were a little surprised. It was one room, with a bathroom, a big king-sized bed, a couch, color TV, and a fireplace. The room smelled like pine trees. "We have to make the most out of it." It was actually pretty cozy; the bed mattress was made out of goose down, as were the pillows and the comforter. We had our own porch with two chairs overlooking the lake. "This is romantic," Lori said. Cabin Number 9 became our getaway place for our alone time from then on, even though it was five hours away from our homes. While we were staying there, we went canoeing, horseback riding, and shopping. Dinners out in the woods were different then in the big city, the check was a heck of a lot cheaper. The lodge had its own beach and we even swam in the lake. We were having so much fun enjoying each other's company.

In the evenings at the cabin, Lori would make a fire in the fireplace. The nights were full of romantic fantasies that lasted till dawn. It was our time, our alone time. We spoke to each other a lot while we were at the cabin. Mainly about our years in high school together, about some of the stupid things we did, and never getting caught. We also discussed the years to come. Are we going to make it or will events just fall into place to lead us to our destiny? I didn't know, and I don't think Lori did either but she had, what I would call, visions of things from the past and of the present that she always talked about. This didn't happen all the time. Sometimes I called her out on her visions, calling them crazy, but she was serious. She said that we had a connection a long time ago, and that she was drawn to me. She had been telling me this for years, and she also told her close friends and cousins the same thing. I always told her, "I have your back." I just wish I had answers for her. Yes, I told her about my dreams I had in the past of her, such as her and I in a carriage ride together, but then the dream would fade out. The dream would never show me anywhere or anything else except for that carriage ride. Who knows? Maybe someday, when Lori and I leave this earth, we will truly find out what the meaning of that dream was.

Our trip up at Lake George was full of everlasting memories. As we packed up Sunday afternoon we looked at each other with long faces, dreading Monday morning. We both started work, but we knew we would come back. This place we found in the middle of the woods, our *'romantic getaway'* as we called it, would now and forever be a part of our life. And every time we came up here, more memories would be made. I'd like to share a poem with you that Lori gave me that morning:

The wide stretch of moon light, played lightly with the palms, and the softness of the wind matched your kiss. The music from the background faded out when the sea played our song. A fantasy come true, that's me and you, when we're together, anything the earth could bring couldn't be better than a life together with you. Just two, me and you. Love forever, Lori.

Steven Zarycki

LIVING APART: THE SOLUTION

There we were, fresh out of high school, ready to go out into the working world. *Did we make the right choice?* I didn't know, but we were going to find out real quick. What relationship doesn't have its ups and downs? We made money and we saved it for our future; that was the lay of the land. Days turned in to weeks, weeks into months, and months into two years. Lori was working as a dental assistant. I, on the other hand, was working from job to job, finding out the hard way. We were still both living at home. We still went on long, interesting drives, staying at hotels, making adventures, and enjoying each other's company. There were times that Lori and I had arguments. One argument almost ended our relationship, but we found out that talking was the best medicine and it only made us stronger. When Lori and I went to family functions with relatives we were always the center of attention. Questions were constantly being drilled into us from both sides of the family. "When are you two getting married?" or "When are you going to get her a ring?" were questions always directed to me. Deep down inside, Lori and I would know when the time was right. We were having fun still. It wasn't so bad living at home, but the time would come when we would move out and start our life together. I didn't know when that would be, but it would be soon.

My father came to me one day. He knew I was struggling to find a steady job that paid well. I really had no career path that I wanted to follow. He asked me if I wanted to work with him at the bank. My father was in charge of a bank near our house; so this wasn't a bad deal. "Sure," I told him. It would be nice to wear a suit and tie for once instead of jeans. The job at the bank wasn't too far from my parents' house either. It was about thirty miles, so the commute was worth the money I was going to make. Now that both of us had steady jobs, I made sure I was putting money away for Lori and I, for our future.

It was tough living in separate houses even though we only lived about a hundred yards apart from each other. Some nights, Lori and I would sneak over to each other's houses. I would climb inside her house through her bedroom window.

I used to hide a small step ladder in the bushes so I could sneak in. One morning, I broke the screen outside her window as I was sneaking out to head home from spending a night with Lori. Her parents found out a couple of months later. Her father, Tony, was pissed but thought it was funny. He confronted me and said, "Why don't you use the front door next time." Lori's parents knew what type of love we shared and eventually so did my parents. At least now we didn't have to tell them where we were going. We were adults and we made our own decisions.

On weekends, it was just the two of us all the time. Our love was so strong, and sometimes our eyes would tear up because we had to say goodnight. One night, Lori was tapping on my window at 1:30 a.m. I said to her, "Are you nuts walking here in the dark?" "Well, you did it," she said. "But I am a guy!" I told her. My room was downstairs on the first floor, so we were safe from anybody hearing us. "Let's just leave and live together. We can afford it. With you here at your house, and me at my house, it's tough," Lori said. We made love that night, but during that time, I was taking into consideration what Lori mentioned before. I didn't want her to be unhappy. I walked her home that night, and I told her I would see her after work, giving her a kiss goodbye. I thought a lot over the next couple of days, and I made the biggest decision of my life; one that I would never regret. I went to the local jewelry store in town one day after work and bought the engagement ring. It was a beautiful-looking ring. It was one large stone surrounded by smaller stones, about 2.5 carats. We went looking at rings from time to time when we went shopping, so I already knew what type of ring style she liked and what her ring size was. It was four days before Easter. I think we went to a disco to dance and drink. She asked me, "Did you think about what I said the other night?" "Yes, I did," I told her. "Give me till Good Friday," I added. I knew I couldn't tell her I had a ring for her, so I had to lie to her. I told her the Friday paper had a big listing on apartments, so we would be able to look for an apartment in there. She was happy to hear that. But I made a mistake. Lori noticed that there was a jewelry bag in the back seat of my car. Thank God it was empty. I told her that I had found the empty bag in my house and I used it to store my lunch for work. She accepted my answer with a puzzled look on her face. She knew I was lying. She wasn't stupid. We went home after the disco club and I gave her a kiss goodnight. I arrived at home and she called me within ten minutes asking me again about the jewelry bag and the apartments. She told me she couldn't wait till Good Friday for a decision. I said, "You have to. I will see you in the morning, honey."

Well, the day had come. Good Friday, 1983. A big day. A very special day. *Was I nervous?* Not at all! If I could, I would have married Lori freshman year; but of course that was impossible. We experienced a lot of growing up since we were fourteen years old. Our love was that of *old love*. It was like we had loved before, in a previous time in history, and we found each other again. But it would be a new love, with new experiences, once I gave her the ring. This is the woman I wanted to spend the rest of my life with. No doubt about it. I told my parents in the morning that I was going to propose to Lori. They wished me off and said, "Good luck, son. We love you."

I walked over to Lori's house, and rang the doorbell. Lori answered the door with a smile. I told her I wanted to talk to her father. "He's in the family room," she said nervously. I turned my back for a moment, looked around, and Lori was nowhere to be found. She apparently ran into her room. I must have said something and she became upset. I wasn't really sure. However, I had to keep on moving forward and talk with her father. I saw him sitting in his comfortable chair watching television. I took a deep breath, and I said, "Good morning, Pop." "What's up young man?" he said. "Listen, I want your permission to…," and before I could say anything else, he said "Well, it's about time." He picked himself up off the chair, shook my hand, and then gave me a big hug. Then, he proceeded to yell, "Jo Ann, come here!" She came running from the back room. "What Tony?!" she said, with a concerned smile. "Meet your new son-in-law," he replied to her. Jo Ann gave me a kiss and a hug. I finally was able to get a word out of my mouth and I asked them both, "Do you think she'll say yes?" They laughed. "Are you kidding?" "You know where she is, go ask her." I walked to the back of the house to Lori's room. When I opened the door Lori was standing there, staring at me. Before I could even get two words out of my mouth she took the ring and put it on her finger. I didn't even get to kneel on one knee. She was overcome with joy and happiness. She was full of emotion. She jumped on me, gave me a huge bear hug and kiss, and said, "Now you know you were the one!" Lori was so happy. It's so difficult to explain it. After all we've been through, good and bad, our dream came true for her and me. Lori and her mother wasted no time. They both jumped on the telephone and called the relatives, and I guess my mom was doing the same thing at our house as well. What a wonderful moment that was.

That night, Lori and I celebrated in our traditional way by dining at our favorite restaurant in New York. Afterwards, it was our alone time together. It was the most romantic night of our lives. Soft words were spoken almost at a whisper, where we could hear our hearts beating as one; it was so perfect. Lori's eyes were closed as if she was dreaming. I asked her what she was thinking about, and she said, "The day you and I met, you took my hands and put them up in the air, and you grabbed my waist and you looked into my eyes. I was filled with so much emotion at that moment. I was wishing you would kiss me, and you did, and you did it with such passion that I knew you were the one I was to marry. Steven, when you kissed me it sparked a past that you and I had together, an old love, whether you believe me or not. I don't know who I was or who you were back then, but we're back together again to share our love as one!" I whispered back to her, "I do believe that we were together in another time, like we were meant to be, and something deep inside of each one of us brought our souls together." Lori hugged me so tight that night. We traveled home with the sun rising. I brought her to her house, gave her a kiss, opened the car door for her, walked her to her front door, and said goodbye. My dad was awake when I arrived home. Being the character that he was, he said to me, "I guess it was a late night celebration for you two. Are you ok?" he asked me. "Yes," I said back to him with a smile. "I'm going to take a nap."

Easter morning came. Lori and I went to church, her arm clinched under my arm. She was so content that morning with the ring on her finger and a flower on her chest; she was proud to be my future wife. She can actually call me her fiancé now, and I thought that was amazing. Father Frank, who performed the Easter Mass that morning, came over to us to give us an Easter blessing. Lori showed him the ring, he was happy for both of us. He would later be the priest to witness our wedding ceremony. After mass, we enjoyed ourselves at Easter celebrations at both households, and of course, *every* relative wanted to see the ring and congratulate us. We had to just go with the flow. Johanna, Lori's grandmother, was very overwhelmed with emotions that day because Lori was her closest grandchild, and now she would be leaving the nest. Towards the end of the day, we were both exhausted, and just wanted to get away for a couple of hours and sleep. We stayed at a local hotel and we fell asleep. When we woke up, it was 9:30 at night. For a minute, we both panicked. Then I said, "We don't have to go anywhere, we don't have a curfew." Lori replied, "Your right." We both started to laugh. That was one of the best feelings in the world for us, knowing that we didn't have to rush home to each other's house to explain where we were to our parents. We decided to stay the night there, have our alone time together, and talk

about our future wedding ceremony.

Lori and I did a lot of things together from the time we first met. We truly learned everything and anything about each other. We grew up together, knowing about each other's good side, and the bad. And, we worked together to achieve the same goal in our relationship. We trusted each other, respected each other, and most of all, we *loved* each other. Why get married if you don't love each other? You see, love, in my opinion, is a friendship that catches fire, and it never dies out. It is quiet understanding, mutual confidence, sharing, and forgiving. It is loyalty through moral and immoral times. It settles for less than perfection and makes allowances for human weaknesses. Love is content with the present, it hopes for the future, and it doesn't fret over the past. It's the day-in and day-out story of frustrations, compromises, disappointments, victories, and working towards common goals. If you have love in your life, it can make up for many things you lack. If you don't have it, no matter what else there is, it's not enough.

THE BIG DAY

Let the wedding planning begin. Lori and I wanted the wedding at this place called The Fiesta, located in Wood-Ridge, NJ. Every time we drove by The Fiesta, Lori would always say, "This is where I want our wedding." Lori's parents, Lori, and I all traveled to The Fiesta to check it out and make the reservations. Lori's mother lit a cigarette before going inside; she was so nervous about the whole wedding. The lead time on the hall was two years, so we agreed to the terms and Lori's father signed and dated the wedding: July 20, 1985. We now had two years to save money by working our butts off, plan the entire wedding, and make sure that everything was covered before the big day. I was getting a headache just thinking about it. However, Lori was excited for the whole thing. She was the busy little bee of the entire wedding planning process. She was constantly on the move, always looking here and there for ideas for our wedding. "Let's check out this photographer!" she said, or "Let's go look at this place, and this place!" I was so overwhelmed and exhausted. Thank God for the weekends.

The first party we had before our big day was an engagement party at her parent's house. What a nice affair they gave us! There were numerous guests, people that I didn't even know, and countless gifts for us to enjoy. All of the gifts of course were going towards a new house. *House?* I thought to myself, *Holy Crap! We were still living at home*! This was all for a house we clearly didn't have yet. Time to start looking for a place to live by wedding time.

Currently, I was still working for my father. He was preparing to build a new branch of his banking company in a town located in South Jersey named Forked River. While he was building the foundation for the bank, my father's friend George, who owned a real estate company, expressed to my father that there was a house for sale on the market down in that area. The house was located on the water, what Lori always wanted, and would be a great location for the two of us. We decided to take a weekend trip to Forked River to scout this place out. When we arrived at this house, we were awestruck. It was a ranch-style house with waterfront property. A perfect location to raise a family and have get-togethers, plus it had a dock for a boat. However, the place needed a ton of renovation work. I didn't care, I was pretty skilled with my hands. I had "rose-colored glasses," and Lori knew it. I could tell in her eyes that she wanted this place, and I did too. We brought her parents to see it; they didn't say very much. They didn't see the potential this place could bring us. All they kept saying was that it needed a ton of work, but we didn't care. Facing another life-changing decision, on April 1, 1984 I closed on the property. My parents gave Lori and me the down payment as a wedding gift; that really meant a great deal to me. I couldn't believe what was actually happening to me in my life at that moment: buying a house, planning a wedding, working full time, and helping Lori with whatever she wanted, all before I turned 24 years old. I sensed the grey hairs coming in fairly quickly.

    Thankfully, the Forked River branch of my father's banking company opened up early. There was no way I was commuting every day from Upper Saddle River to Forked River. I decided to start living at the house I just purchased, which had no furniture and a lot of crap to remove from the previous owners. I found a couch that wasn't being used at parent's house, so I brought it down to Forked River with me one day, and that became my bed for the time being. Lori would travel down every weekend to help out with renovations, such as tearing down walls, cleaning debris, and other various projects that needed to be completed. If you can name any task that a first-time homebuyer performs on their house, Lori did it. Some weekends we took a break from demolishing, but time was not on our side. We had to get our wedding party picked out; this was completed in about a day. The total amount of people was fifteen, including Lori and I. She wanted a rainbow wedding with different colored dresses for her bridesmaids and matching usher's ties and cummerbunds for the groomsmen. Invitations had to be mailed and tuxes had to be fitted, but Lori had some good luck on her side. The wedding dress that she picked out didn't have to be sized, it fit perfectly. Things were falling into place slowly, even though we had a little more than a year to do things. I wanted everything to go as smooth as possible for Lori. Eventually, the year flew by.

    With all this wedding planning and house remodeling we still had time for ourselves, which meant a lot for the two of us. There were days of high anxiety and mental anguish, but we managed it the best we could. We wanted to do everything all by ourselves so it would be right…and we did. Lori would say, "Boy, time flew by!" "Yes it did!" I would repeat back to her. I asked her a stupid question one morning, "Do you still want to marry me after all we've been through?" "More than anything else in the world!" she exclaimed. "Why do you ask me?" "I don't know, I am just making sure" I told her. She said, "You're just nervous." "Aren't you?" I replied back. "Hell yes!" she fired back. Why should we be nervous? This is what we wanted for a long time. I guess we just wanted to make sure everything went right.

Time for the bridal shower. We received gifts from our parents, grandparents and friends. Lori was so elated, I couldn't have been happier for her. Her dreams in the love letters to me from high school were coming true. It was like our very own fairy tale. After the party, we had some downtime for a few days. We transported all of the presents to our house in Forked River. Every room was set with furniture, pictures were scattered on every wall, new carpets were installed, rooms freshly painted, and our master bedroom suite was complete. However, we didn't dare sleep in the master suite until after the wedding because we were told it was bad luck. We used the pullout bed; it did the job quite well. Finally catching a break from our hectic lives, we sat back and cuddled on the couch in the living room of our new home. Lori sat next to me. She had one of my work t-shirts on with no pants, her wavy blond hair and her makeup just right. God, I was blessed. Only He could have given me an angel like her. We had a beautiful night alone together.

The next day, Lori and I woke up and decided to review the wedding criteria before tomorrow's wedding rehearsal. We had to make sure who had to be paid for what and who was taking care of this and that. This took about an hour or so. Planning a wedding is like flying a space shuttle. You have to know what you're doing, or you're going to crash and burn. You have to be positive that everything is going to go as planned. After all the stressful planning and making sure people were paid, we checked around the outside and inside of the house to make sure we didn't leave anything on or water running. We packed our suitcases for our honeymoon, put the suitcases in the car, and locked the house up. We would be coming back in two weeks as husband and wife. That was exciting for us. For almost nine years, Lori and I waited for this day. What we experienced at such a young age of fourteen to now can only be written in a book and shared with others. There's only truth that can be spoken about our relationship together. Whether she came to me or I came to her didn't matter anymore, because we will be one in the same. As we drove away from the house, Lori asked me what I was thinking about. "Just dreaming," I said. "Anything good?" she asked back. "Just about the whole journey we've shared together so far." From a distance, I could see our house in the rearview mirror. I was so anxious to get back home with my future wife, to begin our lives together.

    Wedding rehearsal day. All that hard work of planning would come to an end for both of us. The big day was tomorrow. I had to get my hair cut, pick up the tuxes, pick up the flowers, and get ready for the rehearsal dinner. I drove to Lori's parents' house, picked her up, and traveled to rehearsal. The rehearsal went on without a hitch. Father Frank was going to preform our ceremony with one other priest from my Catholic church and Lori's reverend from her church. Father Frank was a good friend growing up, we played racquetball together. He was a great mentor and teacher, keeping me on the right track in life. We presented our gifts to our ushers, bridesmaids, and parents. The night finally came to an end. Lori and I spent every minute together before the stroke of midnight. We shared a drink, a kiss and a hug, and I said, "I'll see you tomorrow afternoon, Mrs. Zarycki!" She paused for a minute, and said, "That's beautiful."

    Wedding day finally arrived. I couldn't wait to phone my soon-to-be-wife when I woke up, but my mother didn't let me. My mother came over to me and whispered in my ear, "It's your wedding day!" I had fallen asleep under our baby grand piano that night because all the couches were taken by the relatives staying over. It was around 8:00 AM in the morning and it was a hot day outside, around 90° or so. My brothers were already setting up the bar outside, tuxes were handed out to all the groomsmen, and delicious food was cooking on the stove for the after church party. I was so nervous I couldn't even eat breakfast. I did manage to get a beer down to calm my nerves and take a shower. When I finished with my shower, everyone was dressed and ready to go except for me. I had to rush to get ready or I was going to be late to my own wedding. All the groomsmen had black pants and white tuxes with bow ties and cummerbunds to match all the bridesmaids' dresses. Real classy, I would say. We were all ready to head towards the church. We packed ourselves into the limos, grabbed more liquor and beer for the ride over, and began our journey to the ceremony.

Arriving at the church, which was only down the road from the house, I walked out of the limo to one of the back rooms of the church with my brother Tom, who was the best man, and the priest, Father Frank. I had to say my confessions before the wedding; I remember having a long conversation. Just kidding! It was short and sweet, and then it was off to the main chapel. I could see that the church was packed with so many friends and relatives on both sides of the family. My mother and father were in their assigned pews already. My future mother-in-law was in her seat as well. Both sets of grandmothers were also in their seats. It was such a beautiful sight; two families coming together as one. People from both sides were giving me thumbs up from afar. That made me feel relaxed, but truthfully, I wasn't. I was nervous, sweating profusely through my tuxedo. I wanted to see my bride. Once I see her, I knew my life would be complete. The ushers were ready in the back of the church, all lined up with their bridesmaids. I caught a glimpse of Lori, just the back of her. "Wow!" I said, padding away the sweat from my forehead. I glanced at my mother and Lori's mother. I took a big breath, and then the organist started to play. One by one, the ushers and bridesmaids came down the aisle, then our flower girl, my cousin Linda, and then Kathi, Lori's sister, who was the maid of honor. The organist transitioned to the entrance song, 'Here Comes the Bride'. Here Lori comes, down the aisle, with her father. I wanted to run down the aisle and pick her up and start spinning her around with our lips embraced, but I couldn't move. There she was, with a beautiful smile. She was an angel sent from God to marry me. My high school sweetheart. My soul mate. Her father slowly pulled back her veil, gave her a kiss, turned to me, shook my hand firmly, and gave me Lori's hand. She squeezed my hand tightly and gave me a little wiggle with her finger. She was just as nervous as I was. It was a full mass. It seemed like hours went by, but it was only an hour wedding mass. We performed our own vows. I started first and said to her, "Lori,

I love you as you are, and will always love you for whatever you become. I will learn to use my heart to provide you the love that you need, the caring and support you need, till death do us part. I love you." Then Lori said her vows. I wish I could remember what she said that day, but I know she meant every word. Then, we exchanged rings and finally, "You may kiss the bride" was said by Father Frank. It was a small kiss. Lastly, the next saying we'd been waiting for finally came. We had been waiting for all of the nine years we knew each other. Father Frank, with much enthusiasm, said, "May I now introduce, for the first time as husband and wife, Mr. and Mrs. Steven Zarycki."

    We strolled down the aisle as fast as we could to the back of the church so we could embrace ourselves in our private time before the wedding attendees started filing out. It was a quick embrace, a long kiss, and a thank you to each other for our dream that came true. After church, everybody went to my parents' house for an after-church party before the reception. Lori, me, and the rest of our wedding party had our pictures taken. There were so many pictures taken that I was starting to see random flashes throughout the day. On the way to the reception, it was only Lori and I in the limousine with a bottle of champagne. It took about a half-hour to drive to The Fiesta from the church. During that drive it was all about us. Kisses upon more kisses, laughing and smiling at each other all the way to the reception. We even drove past an old hotel we used to visit when we were younger. We didn't have to visit those anymore, we had our own home now. Honestly, I think if we had more time we would have 'done it' in the limo, but we saved that for later.

    We arrived at The Fiesta. We really didn't want to go inside; we wanted to be alone. The entire wedding day seemed to be flying by fast, but it really wasn't. Lori and I exited the limo and were whisked away to our private room. There, Lori and I shared various appetizers and champagne. I made sure our door was locked so Lori and I wouldn't be disturbed. About an hour later there was a knock on the door. It was one of the workers at The Fiesta explaining to us it was time to see everybody in the reception ballroom. We can finally share that long-awaited time together as husband and wife. We heard the maître d' announcing all the ushers and bridesmaids, and sooner than later it would be our turn. Lori was on one side of the stairs, while I was on the opposite side. Then our announcement came. We walked down the stairs, met in the middle of the long staircase, exchanged a kiss and a hug, and then walked down the center staircase together as husband and wife. After the huge applause and cheers, we danced the first song together on the ballroom floor. Our first dance as husband and wife was to the music of "Through the Eyes of Love", which was the theme song from the movie *Ice Castles*. What a beautiful moment that was. I whispered in Lori's ear, "I love you with all of my heart. You had no choice this time to be the first one on the dance floor, did you?" She laughed and smiled, and we kissed. She answered, "I don't want this moment ever to end!" I voiced to her, "This is only the beginning to a long life together."

The reception was going extremely well. There was food, live music, dancing, and of course, drinking. Lori's father even paid for an extra two hours of open bar and live music because nobody wanted to leave. There must have been more than 250 plus guests. The wedding reception lasted until around 1:15 AM. Lori and I really didn't get to eat much or enjoy the festivities like everyone else. We were too busy running around greeting relatives. We needed chap stick by the end of the night from all the kissing we were doing to each other. People kept tapping their wine glasses, so we had to kiss every time. We had some quality time with the photographer outside the reception as well. He allowed us to perform our own poses. Each pose was personal and showed our true love to each other, especially one picture of me sitting on a pillar with Lori embracing my shoulders giving me a kiss. It looked like a heart formed in between us. The photographer was finally done taking pictures and left us to go back inside the reception. Having a brief private moment together, we found a secluded spot outside the hall. She put her arms around my neck; I put my arms around her waist. I drew her close towards my body, and we kissed. At that single moment again, our hearts beat as one. The lights were dimmed yellow. I opened my eyes to look at her kissing me. What a beautiful wife I had, with her warm skin glowing with everlasting love, as if she was in a dream and didn't want to wake up. It lasted for five minutes, and in those five minutes it lasted a lifetime. My cousin Stephanie found us, and like little kids we were told to get back upstairs for the sendoff. We walked up to the main table which overlooked the vast gathering of family and friends. The band started playing the sendoff song. We started waving our hands toward everyone and a sea of hands rose from the sides of each individual as they waived back. We slowly stepped backwards and the curtain drew close. We said our goodbyes to our parents, thanking them for the beautiful wedding they provided us and for letting us experience our lives in our own way. Our limo driver drove us to our hotel which was only a few miles from the hall. We went upstairs to the hotel club first, not even to our room yet. There was a party going on as well, we couldn't escape it. After staying for about an hour, we looked at each other and nodded our heads signifying "It's time to go." We said good night to everyone, and retired to our hotel room. It was almost 3:00 in the morning. Our plane was taking off at 9:00 AM for our honeymoon trip, so we needed to sleep. We arrived at the door to our room, noticing a trail of passed-out bodies scattered along the floor of the hotel hallway. Who had our key? I sure didn't. My brother had to call the front desk for someone to open the door for us. Lori had been on her feet all day, so I carried her in my arms while waiting for the hotel employee to arrive. She put her arms around my neck and her head on my shoulder. Finally, the employee came and the door was open; I carried her in and kicked the door shut. I placed her on the bed, and removed my tuxedo jacket. I kneeled by her side and removed her shoes. "Thank you!" she said to me. "For what?" I asked. "For becoming my husband." We now had are alone time again. However, we were so tired we fell asleep. We were startled by a knock at the front door. "Lori! We over slept!" I yelled. Thank God our luggage was packed, and our clothes were out. It was a quick change, makeup, and coffee, and we were off to the airport.

I had never been on an airplane in my life, but Lori was a seasoned traveler. I had to cross myself before I stepped onto the airplane. Here we go. The airplane started down the runway, with the nose of the plane lifting off the ground. There was a slight bang, then another large, deep-sounding bang. The nose of the airplane came down, the engines were thrown into reverse and the airplane came to an immediate halt. The doors flew open, and the slide chutes came out. We were instructed by the flight attendants not to panic and slide down the chutes to the runway. We walked to waiting buses in the middle of the runway, and they brought us over to the terminal. Everything happened so fast, Lori and I had no time to react. We found out on the way to the terminal that the tires blew out, and if we had lifted off, we would've had to land on foam on the runway in Orlando, Florida. What a terrific, terrifying first time in an airplane that was! "Now what?" we said to ourselves. We had to wait for the airplane to come from Miami to Newark to take us to Orlando. A four hour delay. "Can you believe this?" I said to Lori. "What can you do?" she replied. She was able to find a payphone and call her parents to tell them about our situation. They contacted the limousine company in Florida and told them about the delay. While waiting, I kept telling Lori I didn't want to get back on that airplane, or any airplane. She ordered me to calm down. She gave me a kiss and hug, and told me not to worry. "Have a drink!" she said. "Or have a couple of them. You need to get the edge off." Lori and I, before the fiasco, had met a couple on the plane celebrating 10 years of marriage. We told them it was our honeymoon. We found them at the airport bar. We began talking and drinking, all four of us having a great time. Finally, the other airplane was here and it was time to board. This time the plane took off with no errors and we were airborne. Lori had to use the ladies room while in flight. I waited a minute or two, walked over to the restroom she was in and knocked on her door. "What do you want?"

she said with a smile. I was laughing. "Can I fit in there?" I said. She looked at me, gave me a little flirty gesture, and I went in. She propped onto the sink, while I sat on the toilet and then she stood up in front of me. Alone time again. I don't know how we 'did it' without making noise, but we did it. It was an interesting experience. You only live once, right? We were now part of the "mile high club" as some people would say. Half the people on the plane knew we were just married; Lori had a corsage on her chest and a flower in her hair from the wedding. We had smiles on our faces coming out of the bathroom. We were in love and we didn't care. What can I say? People have been making love since the beginning of time.

    Finally, the plane landed and we said our goodbyes to the people we met. The limo picked us up out front and drove us to the resort for two weeks of fun and sun. We were staying at one of the newer resorts in Orlando where we had a suite. We opened the door to the suite and I carried Lori in and laid her down on the bed. There, in the middle of the room, was a bottle of champagne with flowers and balloons. Lori read the card; apparently it was from all the people we met on the airplane. The couple we had made friends with arranged it for us. It was a nice way to start our honeymoon. The days went by slow, and each one was full of activities. If we weren't at the pool or at the park, we were shopping. We made a lot of friends, whether it was playing volleyball by the pool, having fine cuisine at dinner, or dancing the night away. The nights were for us, our alone time. I have to state that dancing was a romantic part of the experience, especially the slow dances with my arms around Lori's waist and her arms around my neck. I don't think there was enough room to fit a credit card between us while we danced. At one of our restaurants, I requested our wedding song, "Through the Eyes of Love". The live band played it. They also announced to everyone in the restaurant that we were newlyweds. We heard sounds of clapping and cheering. Lori became embarrassed and buried her face into my shoulder. After dinners and dancing, at night we would take long walks in our bare feet around the man-made lake. I carried her shoes. Small conversations were spoken, and we exchanged kisses throughout the walks. Then we would retire to the room where we were really alone and, like the first-time together, it seemed to last forever, night after night.

The evening before we were about to travel back home, I ordered dinner to be set up in the room; Lori had no clue this was going to happen. I decided to take her shopping and told the front desk at the resort that we would be back at the room around 7 PM. We spent the last beautiful day in sunny Florida spending money here and there, buying up items we could bring back with us on the airplane. At five minutes before 7 PM, we arrived back at our hotel room suite. Lori opened the door slowly and suddenly her mouth dropped to the floor. There were lit candles placed all around the room. There was also a small round table with white linen and two chairs in the middle of the suite. On the table were white lilies, Lori's favorite flower, and off to the side there was champagne in a silver bucket with ice. Our dinner, which was surf and turf, was still hot and fresh from the kitchen. Finally, there was a card from me to her on the table as well. The lights were dimmed, and a machine that produced a white mist on the ground was hooked up in the corner of our room. The machine also projected a scene from an enchanted forest all around the entire room. Boy, room service did their job right for me! Lori just kept saying, "Oh my god, how did you do this?" I replied with a smirk, "I had help from little leprechauns." Lori turned around and ran over to me from the center of the room. She nearly knocked all the packages from my arms. She hugged me so tight. We kissed and started spinning in place. My eyes were fixated on her. It was as if she was in a dream world, and didn't want it to end. I asked her if she wanted to take a bath before dinner and she said, "No, we can eat first." "Are you sure?" I asked. As I opened the bathroom door, she glimpsed in. In the bathroom there were candles lit all around, the smell of rose petals wafting up from the Jacuzzi. "Oh my god!" she gasped, "When did you find time?" Again, I said to her, "I had help from my leprechauns." That's all it took. She stripped off her clothes quickly, put one foot in the tub, then the next foot, and slowly immersed her body into tranquility. Lori asked me if I wanted to come in. I said, "No, you enjoy this." "Ah, come on in, please!" she said in a playful manner. I couldn't say no again, so I removed my clothes as well and slipped in. That water was steaming hot, but also relaxing. I was worried dinner was getting cold, but realized I had forgotten that the food was on warmers. So, we took our time in the Jacuzzi. "Wash my back," she said, "and don't get my hair wet." Then she said to me, "Wash my feet and my legs." "Hey, what am I?" I inquired to her. "You're my husband, my soul mate, my prince" she said. That's all I needed to hear; I was like soft butter after that. An hour passed, and my fingers were almost starting to prune. We were so oily when we stepped out of the Jacuzzi that the towels didn't even dry us off. I grabbed Lori, taking both her hands with my left hand, put them above her head, and with my right hand, I placed it around her waist, drawing our bodies closer together. I let go of her hands, and they slowly dropped around my neck drawing my lips closer to hers. What a moment that was. "You remembered," she said. Three hours later, we ate our dinner, and went to sleep. A perfect way to end our honeymoon.

Stairways

STARTING OUR LIFE TOGETHER

Saturday afternoon we returned to our home in Forked River to a house filled with people waiting to get a glimpse of the newlyweds. Relatives were snapping pictures left and right of me carrying Lori through the front door. We had a little get-together with some food and drinks. After that was all over, everyone left our house and it was finally quiet. It was now time for our lives to begin. That night was our first night at home together as husband and wife. "Honey," I said. "Do you want to go out to eat?" "No," she said, "Let's order take-out and be comfortable." We had no problem with take-out. We ordered Chinese food because we didn't have it while we were on our honeymoon, and Lori had a craving for it. We laid down in bed, ate our Chinese food, and watched our wedding video that my mother-in-law had dropped off. It was a little comical in the beginning, with me acting like an idiot at my house before the ceremony began. But then it turned serious yet heartwarming, especially the scenes with us showing how much in love we really were and how nervous we were that morning. We told each other while we watched the tape that we weren't really that nervous, but movies don't lie, and we justly were. The wedding video showed our true colors; it showed how true we were to ourselves. After watching the video, I looked at Lori. She had tears in her eyes. "What's the matter honey?" I asked. She said, "I want to relive that entire day with you." When she said that to me my heart filled with more happiness than you could imagine. "We will each year with our anniversary, and when there's a year you want to renew our vows, will do it," I stated to her firmly. She moved her food aside. I did the same. I dimmed the lights. I walked slowly to her, gave her a hug, and rolled her on top of me. She slowly bent down to kiss me and whispered in my ear that she was the luckiest woman in the world to have me as her husband and her soul mate. I whispered back to her, "I knew from the beginning that you were the one for me, that somehow, if it was in another time when we shared a love together, this time it will last forever. I love you, Lori."

That first weekend home as husband and wife flew by quickly. Sunday morning we went to church, then immediately after we traveled down to Cape May to walk around and enjoy the little shops. We found a café for lunch, which was on the ocean. We sat out in the sun to relax and then prepared ourselves for Monday. That morning, I woke up, took a shower, got dressed, and gave her a kiss goodbye. She was still in bed; she didn't have a job at the moment, but that was okay. She wanted to concentrate on the house to make it her own. Lori, at the least, wouldn't be home alone. She had a dog, a black lab named Rocky. Lori had picked him up when he was a puppy before we were married. He was older now and was a very obedient dog. The only thing I didn't enjoy about him was that he sometimes cut into our alone time. Rocky was always on our bed, lying there all day spread-eagled. If I closed the door to our bedroom and he was on the other side, he would bark non-stop until the door was opened and he was let in. Ultimately, I became use to his antics and compromised with Lori, agreeing to keep him around. I had to learn to share my time with him; Lori loved animals.

Days turned into weeks, and weeks turned into months. We enjoyed living on our own, especially Lori, who grew accustomed to cooking in her kitchen and making our house a real home. Lori was an amazing cook. I don't think I ever had the same dish twice in one month. On occasion, we would go out to eat and drink, but that was expensive. We liked to save money when we could, and ultimately Lori didn't mind cooking at all. When we had company come over, she would aim to cook these extravagant meals that you could see being served at the Four Seasons restaurant. There were numerous side dishes, meats, fish, and even desserts. No wonder I packed on weight over the years; I couldn't get enough of her cooking.

Finally, after a long extensive search in the Ocean County area of New Jersey, Lori found a job at a dental practice in Brick as an Office Manager. It was about twenty miles from the house and wasn't such a bad gig. It provided great pay, and good benefits. She was home before I came home, usually around 5:00 PM, just in time for her to whip up a tasty meal for me to try.

When I had some free time after work, I would continue fixing up the house. I had finished renovating all three bedrooms, kitchen, bathroom, and dining room. There was one room left, and that was the family room, located towards the back of the house near the water. The roof covering the family room would leak every single time it rained. The home inspectors must have missed it at inspection time before we bought the house. I remember putting pots and pans all over the room in order to catch the rain. We spent a little money towards the repairs, and once they were complete, we could finally start to really enjoy our humble abode. The outside of the house was the main reason why we purchased it in the first place. It was waterfront property; a luxury we never experienced before. We had a dock, a small private beach, and property to expand the house. The only thing we were missing was a boat. However, it didn't take me long to find one on sale through a neighbor, then everything was complete.

Lori and I were enjoying the time we had with each other those few years before having children. Whether it was going on day trips or weekend getaways, we were having fun with each other, always romancing. Whether it was dining out or even just sitting in the backyard, we were enjoying life. Now, I have to admit, there were times when we got ahead of ourselves, like most newlyweds, which placed us in a financial slump. When we looked back on when it all started, we said to each other how lucky we were to experience what we were offered in life.

Lori and I, that was it. Lori and I, all through our lives together from the first day we met. We had friends, but not to socialize or go out with. They were friends we met in our travels and at work. Lori and I did everything together morning, noon, and night. The only time we were a part was when we worked. Some people would say it wasn't healthy, but to Lori and I that didn't bother us. It just felt natural to be by ourselves. We weren't loners. We were always talking and on occasion would argue, but it always resolved itself in one way or another. When Lori and I were younger we would always talk. For us, talking was the best medicine in our relationship, no doubt about it. We always said, "Take one day as it comes, life's too short."

As time went on, things kept pretty much the same. My wife always looked beautiful; always pampering herself as most woman do, getting her hair done at least once a month, nails polished, and the occasional facial when the money was there. One thing I loved was when she would take her extensively long baths at home. When she placed her bath salts in the water it would make the whole house smell like a garden; it was tranquil and peaceful. She really was an exceptional woman, and she did it all for me. I tried to keep myself up to par with her but, with Lori always cooking great food, I gained a little weight here and there. But, working on the house would help me lose a little weight also, so I was still pretty fit.

When the holidays came Lori and I would put up a tree, decorate the house, and then go to New York to see the sights. Lori always loved her Christmas tree ornaments. Decorating the house was something she was always good at, especially during the holiday seasons. We would then come home, open presents, and enjoy the holiday. We didn't give each other a lot during Christmas because we gave ourselves a lot throughout the entire year.

One dreary day during the holiday season, Rocky became very ill. Lori and I rushed him to the animal hospital. Unfortunately, he was now an older dog and there was nothing the veterinarian could do to help him overcome being sick. They had to put him to sleep and Lori was extremely upset. She loved that dog like it was her baby. I tried taking her out to dinner later that night, but she had no appetite. I understood. I kind of missed the old boy and his barking as time went on. Now he is in heaven, probably digging a hole through the clouds to bury his bone instead of in our yard.

A couple of months later, I convinced Lori to take a trip with me. We decided to go to Canada. Lori had never been to Canada. I had been there on many occasions with my parents while I was growing up. My family roots stem back to a monk who was not celibate in the early 1600s in Europe. During the early 1900s most of my relatives migrated through Russia into Canada and settled in various provinces, one being Montréal. Lori was really excited about going. It was about eleven hours of driving from our house at the Jersey Shore. We left on a Thursday morning around 1 AM and arrived in Montréal at about noon time. We took four days to relax and see the sights. It was early springtime, where the days were somewhat warm and the nights were cold. We stayed at a cozy bed and breakfast in old Montréal. The town was French speaking, so at times it was difficult to communicate with the people. Lori loved the French food, the outdoor cafes, and the bakeries. We visited a bakery one morning because Lori wanted some pastries to take back to the hotel for when she had her tea. She went into the bakery and browsed at the selection of mouthwatering pastries. She then asked one of the counter girls for help. The girl spoke to my wife in French and evidently Lori was getting a little frustrated with this girl. I could just tell that this girl knew what Lori was saying and that she understood English. So, I stood back and watched my wife handle herself. Lori took her index finger and said, "Listen bitch, I want one of these, and one of these, and I want them now." Well, I think after what Lori said to that girl that she understood English quite well. I couldn't stop laughing after that. Lori took my hand, like a kid and we left the store. Upon leaving the pastry shop Lori turned to me and said she was sorry for her outburst and that the recent loss of her dog Rocky had her tensed up. After that incident though, Lori and I had an amazing time together for three days. We continued on our sightseeing and had a few more romantic dinners. The trip was over, yet our lives were just about to start.

OUR CHILDREN

One day in March, a couple of months before our two year anniversary, I came home from work and I received a kiss. Lori said, "Hello, how was your day?" There were candles lit at the kitchen table and dinner was ready. "Why are you smiling at me?" I asked. "What's all this for, you pregnant or something?" "Yes!" she exclaimed. "Yes, what!?" I questioned hesitantly. "I'm pregnant!" she said with excitement. "Oh my lord, are you kidding?" "No! I just found out this morning at the gynecologist." I was at a loss for words; I had butterflies in my stomach. We were going to have our first child. I was going to be a dad. "I love you, I love you," I said. Lori replied back with the same phrase. "Relax," she said to me. I thought she was giving birth already. She was already on the phone calling her mom, my mom, grandmother, you name it. It seemed as if everyone in the whole neighborhood was finding out. I was going to be a daddy. A couple of months later, Lori went to the doctor's and found out that she was going to give birth to a little boy. I knew she was hoping for a little girl, but just as long as he or she was healthy, that's all that mattered. Lori said to me, "The baby is due in November, just before Thanksgiving." And all I could think of is at least this gives me enough time to get the nursery ready.

Lori and I made sure that we had some good quality time before the baby was born. We took weekend trips up the Hudson to go through some of the historic mansions from the Victorian era. We also went up to Rhode Island to Mansions Row. *Why you may ask?* It was because Lori was always searching for a bit of the past and I had no problem helping her. We also went upstate to our cabin getaway which brought back memories of the earlier days. We just wanted to enjoy ourselves because we knew that when the baby came, life would be a little different.

The months flew by and Lori had her first baby shower. "This kid's going to be spoiled," I said to myself. He was the first grandson of both families. The little prince they called him. I didn't let Lori pick up a finger. I did most of everything that needed to be done. I would go to work while Lori would stay home to put the finishing touches on the nursery. My wife looked so good when she was pregnant. She still kept her body up to par. I'm not quite sure how she did it all. She was an amazing woman and I had no doubt that she would be an amazing mother. We were still having our alone time, with our getaways and all, until the doctor said no more trips because it was too close to the due date. Lori was overdue, so on November 22, 1987, she got induced. No more than an hour later came our son, Christopher Steven Zarycki, whom was 9 pounds and 6 ounces. Mother and baby were doing fine. I can't tell you how many times I told her I loved her that day. She was the perfect wife, mother, and soul mate that any man could want.

In the coming years, Lori taught me a lot about myself. That in the beginning, when she first met me, she told me that I was chosen for her. I asked, "How?" She said, "It showed in your eyes, it showed a man with a heart, feelings, romantic, strong willed and compassionate." That was a lot for me to handle, and I broke down. She said, "It's ok for a man to show emotions, that's one of the traits I love about you, you weren't afraid to show it." With a new baby on our hands and all the love surrounding our family, I was full of emotions. Though, showing my emotions to Lori was never something I ever really aimed to hide.

Six years had gone by already and the world was changing. Our son was doing well; he was quite a smart six year old. He played soccer, was in cub scouts, and looked just like Lori with his blond hair and blue eyes. He also loved the water, always playing and swimming in the backyard. Lori and I were still able to do our own thing from time to time. Whenever we wanted to get away all we did was pick up the phone and call Grandma. They'd take the baby for the weekend, giving us new parents a break. Sometimes, or should I say most of the time, we took the baby with us. We were big on giving our son as many experiences as we could. The boardwalk, the beach, sites, whether historic or not, we always brought him here and there to learn, understand, and most of all, to have fun.

December 1992. Surprise! "Hey, Steve. I'm pregnant!" Lori said. And like that, child number two was on the way. "How long before you're due, Lori?" I said. The doctors say the baby is due in August. We waited a few months and Lori went to the doctors. They told Lori she was going to have a baby girl. Lori and I were more than excited, a little girl. "Thank you, Lord", I said to myself, "for the perfect family". Lori was overjoyed; she was going to have her little girl.

After I heard the news, I reflected back to the letter she wrote to me in high school, a letter I still have. She wrote that she wanted a perfect family. A little boy, a little girl, and that house on the water. It seemed as if it had all come true. It brought tears to my eyes that I couldn't control. I had to go outside, I didn't want my son to see Daddy cry. He always thought crying meant you got hurt. Tears come with joy as well, which he learned as he got older.

Lori came outside a few minutes later; she gave me a hug and a kiss. She knew why I was crying, she knew me like a book. "It's a gift," she said to me, "your ability to remember the memories, so vivid and detailed oriented. Don't dwell on the past, look at the present as a gift. What you and I had, and still have, you keep that in your heart, and never let go of it." Lori always knew the right things to say. What a woman I had, so understanding and so intelligent. I watched her walk down the stairs to the water's edge, onto the dock were she always loved feeding the swans.

Within the blink of an eye, another baby shower for a girl. My little baby angel has more clothes and I would ever have. A couple weeks later, on August 6, 1993, the exact due date, Lori gave birth to our little girl, Alexis Paige Zarycki, a healthy 8 pounds 6 ounces. The whole family was enthralled. This was the family's first granddaughter on both sides, with blonde hair and blue eyes just like her mother.

Now with two children, I really had my wife on a pedestal. I did practically everything I could to help Lori out with the kids. During the nights, I got up; I let her sleep because I knew she needed the rest. I rocked the babies, changed them, and even gave them a bottle, and I enjoyed doing it. Lori found it funny when I would sometimes take one or two bites of the baby's food when I was feeding them, but those little sausages I used to feed them weren't half bad. On occasion Lori did get up and help me. She had the baby's all day, so I wanted to give her a break during the night. You know women are truthfully special, well deserving to be treated like queens.

Lori went back to work after a couple of months and my Aunt Stephanie, who was disabled after she had cancer, would take care of my children while Lori and I were at work. It was just until it was time for them to be allowed to stay by themselves after the school bus dropped them off at home.

Time was passing by fast. Lori and I were involved with every aspect of our children's lives that we could be. Whether it was being a troop master in scouting, being a dance or soccer mom, and even taking part in parent teacher clubs; if our kids were in it, we had some part in it too. Lori and I also made sure that there was some family time, and a lot of it. Whether it was camping, day trips, weekend trips, or vacations we made sure that those kids of ours had every opportunity to see what was out there, in order to learn and to ask questions if they didn't understand, just like Lori and I had in our younger days. From trips to Maine, to the Caribbean, to various cultural events or sporting events, Lori and I made sure we had quality family time with our kids. Whether it was a day trip or a two week vacation, they always thanked Lori and I for being involved in their lives and that was something we really cherished.

It had been a few years, and Lori and I needed some alone time now. So, we called Grandma and she said no problem. We left for the weekend and we told them we'd be back on Sunday night. They told us to take our time, as we did, and we left to go to the mountains in upstate New York. We took a trip down memory lane to our cabin hideaway. It was storming that weekend and there was a mist over the lake. The air was damp and cold, and rumbles of thunder could be heard in the distance. Lori had it all planned out for that weekend, just like I had it planned out on the last day of our honeymoon. But it was all a surprise to me.

The cabins we stayed at were built in the 1940s; it still had its original owners. The main lodge was like a hunting lodge. It had both old world charm and stuffed animals throughout its walls. Lori was a fire bug; she always liked starting fires in the fireplace. She would put so many logs on the fire that I had to take water and throw it on the fire, just to keep it under control. That was my wife. So in our cabin, she started a fire in the fireplace. She told me to go out and get some coffee and wine. I said, "Sure, anything else you need?" She countered back with an assertive no, and said she'd be waiting for me when I got back. So about a half hour later, I returned to the cabin. I climbed up the stairs to the cabin door. I opened the door. I was surprised and a little choked up. There she was in the corner of the cabin dressed in a silk nightgown ending just above the knees, with high heels on, her makeup just perfect, and her hair just perfect. The fire was going. The window was cracked open to hear the rain falling on the leaves, and on the floor of the cabin two blankets with two pillows. There was a plate with cheese and crackers and fruit to the side, and Lori was holding two glasses. Luckily, I had the wine. She had this flaunty, flirty attitude on. It was incredibly sexy. I was dripping wet from the rain. "I got you a present," she said, "It's in the bathroom, go inside and change." I came out, with silk sleep pants and a muscle shirt. "Pour me a glass of wine," she said, with a "Thank you, honey" as I did it. "Lay down, sweetheart." she told me. It was getting hot in that cabin. Not from the fire, but because she started feeding me grapes like the Romans did back in the day. She told me to close my eyes, she whispered in my ear, "I love you," and she kissed my forehead. God! I said to myself, please don't let this night ever end. But like all nights, it did. Like two teenagers, we were up till the next morning. I didn't want to go home and neither did she. That morning we got out of bed slowly with some messing around before we got dressed. I packed our bags, I picked her up, and I carried her down the stairs to the car. I said to her, "Your carriage, my lady," as I put her down and opened the door. She said, "You said that phrase to me a long time ago." I didn't question what she said. She was always right anyway. *Why is it when you go someplace you never want to go back home?* I don't know. We started our trip back. Then, when we got home, it was back to reality. Things were good though, the kids were great, family and all. Our years were going by fast. I decided, however, to make a change in my life. After years in the banking business, I said thank you to my father for giving me the opportunity, but it was time to move on. So I became a salesman, selling building products. It was a good job, and the money was good; just another new milestone in our lives together.

 I would say it was around the middle of April in 1995. We took the kids to a festival in South Jersey for a day of family fun. As we were walking through the vendor's area I came across a booth for the Mrs. New Jersey pageant. They were looking for contestants for their show that was going to be held at the Atlantic City convention hall in the late fall. Lori looked at me and said, "don't you dare". Well, I did, I signed her up not realizing the work that was involved. I didn't care. My wife was beautiful. She had just as much a chance as everybody else did. All I had to do was to get her some sponsors, pay the entry fee and she was in. Lori had a talent, she could sing. But no talent was required in this competition, only bathing suits and evening gowns. Lori was getting nervous as time was growing near. I had to get a tux because I too was going to be on stage with her for a group dance number. I was a little nervous as well. She got her bathing suit and then she went with her mother to get the evening gown which was a white, full length gown with about ten pounds of sequins sewn onto the dress. At the time of competition, Lori was pampered like a queen; facials, manicures, hair, and makeup oh and yes rehearsals for two days. Everything was included, the hotel and all the meals for both of us. We also got some romance in that weekend, a lot of it. The competition began. There were about sixty women there. My wife was so stunning and beautiful she could have knocked the Statue of Liberty off her pedestal. I don't know how she didn't break a sweat, but she did fantastic. Even though she didn't win, she came in the top twenty. She'll always be a winner in my eyes, for all my life.

Two more years had gone by and it happened again. "You're what?" I asked her. "Honey, I'm pregnant!" "You've got to be kidding me?" "No, sweetheart. It's true." I was elated, but shocked. I was starting to think we needed a bigger house. Lori and I were going to have another addition to our family. We found out, as usual, a couple of months later that it was going to be another boy. However, the money was just not there to move. So we decided to put the crib in Chris's room. I don't think Chris was too happy with what we decided at the time; he wasn't too big on sharing his room with a baby.

The baby was due sometime in October, so we had time to get things arranged at the house. The next couple weeks passed, Lori had a surprise baby shower. She received a lot of baby clothes that had to be stored because we had a lot of baby clothes left from when Chris was an infant. But there was no harm in being flourished with more baby gifts. The time was almost here. We were about to have another baby added to our family of four. Lori went to the doctors on the 24th of October for a sonogram, and then the doctor wanted to see her the next day for a taping. Lori didn't want that, but doctors' orders I guess.

The next afternoon I got a call from Lori; she was crying. "What honey? What's the matter? "And then a parent's worst fear. Something was wrong with the baby. As I tried to calm her down over the phone I could feel a pit in my stomach beginning to blow up like a balloon. "The baby died inside of me!" she said to me, crying uncontrollably. I yelled, "I'm coming for you, stay at the doctor's office." And then she replied not to, and that she had already driven home. "What, he made you drive home!?" Needless to say I was extremely pissed off. I flew home in the car, my emotions running wild. I ran to the front door when I got home. I went inside. Lori was standing in the kitchen. I grabbed her and held her in my arms. I couldn't imagine the pain she felt after carrying our child full term and having to give birth to a dead son. We left for the hospital. She got induced and gave birth to our stillborn son on October 25, 1997. I was hoping, as was Lori, that when the baby came out of her womb, he would start crying. But it wasn't meant to be.

The pain and suffering went on for weeks; it lessened over the next couple of months. Lori's boss at the time, paid for the funeral and the burial. He felt so bad for us. He didn't have any kids of his own yet. Our two kids were told the truth. It was hard to explain that God needed another angel for his choir, that's why he took our son, whom we named Corey. Lori named him. I don't know where she got that name and I wasn't going to ask. For some time after that, Lori and I went to bereavement class for about six months. I went a little while longer after she stopped. I tried my best for her, to do whatever she needed; she needed the rest. Knowing my wife though, she got right back up on her feet; even though the pain was still with her.

It was now December and the holidays were back. Lori was still an emotional train wreck due to the loss of our child. I didn't know what I could do. Then Lori mentioned possibly of getting another dog. At the time, we had a cat named Homie, I know weird name, and a bird named Tweedy. I wasn't sure about having another animal in the house, but anything to make Lori happy again was okay with me. So Lori went searching and finally found the type of dog she was looking for. On December 25th Lori and I surprised the kids with a new collie puppy; she named him Casey. Lori loved that dog so much. She stayed up all night lying in the dog bed with him; little did I know he would become her baby. Now, nothing can replace the loss of a child, that's for sure, but Casey healed Lori in a way I can't really explain.

The years were just going by and life was gaining back some normalcy. Our kids were both older now. They knew if the bedroom door was shut not to disturb mom and dad, but how intimate could we get with the kids in the house. Lori and I had our moments, some good some bad, but we always worked it out. Lori always use to say that if a couple didn't argue a little, there wasn't any real love. One of the funniest things we use to do is hold hands together while racing down the street together. We would start to run side by side to see who would win the race back to the house. Neither of us would let the other one win, because we always wanted to win together.

As time went on Lori took up a new hobby, ghost hunting of all things. She belonged to a paranormal research group in South Jersey. She was pretty good at it too. She had me scared a couple of times with pictures and audio she would capture. Lori always told me don't be scared of the dead, be scared of the living. *Oh how true that is.* Lori had this philosophy on where we go when we die. She always use to say how we are here on Earth to do a job and when that job is done then, and only then, can we go home. "When we go to heaven, we all have something to do when we get there." She always said to me when we were younger that she and I were together in another life. I always believed that. She also said that when she goes to heaven she wanted to welcome all the animals and take care of them while they waited for their owners. Yet she always reassured me of something else as well. She said someday when we die she and I would be together again.

Lori was always searching for some hint of our past; I thought it was like looking for a needle in a haystack at times. She watched the movie Titanic more times than I could ever count, and would pick out details that most people would have missed. On our many vacations, we would stay at Victorian bed and breakfasts instead of regular hotels, because she insisted we were together during that era. She would be at awe with all the furnishings and paintings from that time period. Somewhere there was a missing link in our past, which is why she must have took up her paranormal hobby.

As a husband, I always backed her up with love and support hoping that, someday, she would find that missing link she was searching for. But for now we had our love in this time, one we both cherished. Every day was a new page in our life. Whether it was a good day or a bad day, we learned to deal with it. Some of you are saying to yourselves, 'it's not possible to love twice.' *Do you know?* I sure don't, but that's why we searched for truth and understanding regarding it. *Do any of us really know what happens to us when we die?* I sure don't, but that's the beauty of it. We don't know what paths we're supposed to take in our lifetime, but the meaning of love and the meaning of understanding and learning is all that matters.

One day, Lori was going down the basement stairs and one of the trends broke. She fell to the basement floor. Good thing the kids threw the blankets down to be washed that morning. I ran so quick to her, down the stairs. She was ok. A little shaken up, but no cuts or bruises. I gave her a hug and picked her up. I said to her, "You and I have had this thing about stairs all our lives." She looked up at me and laughed. She put her arms around me and we kissed, then slowly laid back onto the blankets. We looked up, and as we did the kids were looking down at us. "Are you guys, ok?" They asked. "Yes." Lori said, "Close the door, daddy and I want to be alone."

Time just kept flying by. Chris started college in 2006; he went to Virginia Military Institute to study Electrical Engineering. Alexis had just started high school. Time wasn't standing still. Lori and I were so proud of our kids. They were both smart, well-mannered, good looking, and on occasional a little temperamental. *But aren't all kids now and then.* No matter what though, we loved them both. Then came Chris's graduation. He made it through four years with the same honors and GPA he always had, and the next year Alexis graduated high school with honors as

well. It was now 2011, and she was starting college at UNC Charlotte come August. It was hard for Lori to see her little girl grown up so fast; she was her baby girl.

Chris was now working for the government. He came home when he wanted to, even though he was still living here. He had his own life now, with his job and new found friends. It was hard for us to see both our kids growing up. We understood that it was inevitable; and that they both had different paths that they wanted to take in their lives. As parents we could relate to this, because we too knew how it was to make our own decisions. Unfortunately, college wasn't something Lori and I finished. *"Any parent would always want better for their kids."*

Lori and I now had our alone time back. Lori and I spent most of our time driving aimlessly around, going to the casino, taking outings on our boat to our hidden cove at the beach. Fun, simple things together; continuing to build our memories together. We were also working and thinking about what was next for us down the road. Lori kept telling me over and over, "We can't sell this house until you find a job somewhere else." I think we were both getting sick of the weather and the flooding in our state. I always liked the cold, but Lori loved the warmer weather a little bit more. We wanted a warmer climate. We looked from time to time for houses on the computer, from North Carolina on south. We even looked at a small house in the Caribbean once or twice. Lori wanted to wait until Alexis's college graduation in May of 2015 before ever moving.

Mother's Day was slowly approaching. Lori and I would have to make an eleven hour trip to Charlotte, NC to pick up Alexis from college and bring her home for the summer. I'm not sure why our children picked colleges so far away. I think we trained them too well to take on new challenges and adventures, or they just were like Lori and despised the cold.

After Lori and I got back from picking up Alexis on Mother's Day, I would have to make it up to Lori the following weekend. Either take her to dinner or to one of our getaway retreats. In 2011, I took Lori to one of these themed resorts in Pennsylvania. They had themed rooms from jungle experiences to beaches; it was really different. Lori, of course, seized the beach room. There was no carpet in the room, it was all white sand and it had a mini wave pool. The waves from the pool would come up to the bed, which was a triple hammock tied between two palm trees. The mattress was a bed of feathers. What a room. It had ocean sounds and stars that filled the night sky, and the water had a tint of blue that reflected around the room. It was like being in the Caribbean, but with no rain. We enjoyed an open bar and food was brought to us. Best of all, there was no windows or a clock to tell us what time it was. I have a thought before I go on: Time! What is time? Well, when you're with somebody you've loved from such an early age in life, and your growing old together, time seems to go fast, but it really isn't. Time is just a word. For Lori and I, we made our own time together, and each minute in the time that went by was a memory for us. We loved our time together from boyfriend and girlfriend to husband and wife. So, getting back to what I was saying, I thought the room was defiantly a little tacky, but it wasn't bad. It was certainly an experience though.

We spent two days in that room. We even got sunburned. *How you ask?* Well the room had ultra-violent lights all around, just like a tanning bed would have. I guess when you have no clothes on, you get a nasty burn; even in some places you shouldn't. It was our fault though for not reading the warning pamphlet that came with the room. But that was ok, she said she had the best Mother's Day present ever; and of course our cherished alone time.

Some months went by, summer turned to fall and then into winter. It was about three weeks before Christmas in 2011. As a family, we were all busy shopping, setting up the tree, and decorating the house. Lori was baking, like always during this time of year, and I came home from work one day giving Lori a kiss and a hug as I walked through the door. However, something was off. Lori looked a little upset. Even though I pestered her with asking what was wrong for quite some time, she kept telling me she was fine. I knew she didn't like it when I kept badgering her with questions, but I just cared.

Luckily, I had a little spy in the house, my daughter. She talked to me outside, so mommy wouldn't hear. Alexis said, "Dad, Mommy lost her diamond from her engagement ring, and told me not to tell you." She said, mommy was crying all day and didn't know what to do. I told Alexis not to say anything; I'll take care of it. All I needed was for her to get me the ring before Christmas Eve. So Alexis did her job. I took the ring to the jeweler and got her a new stone; the jeweler said the prong broke off and the diamond fell out. It probably fell into the cookie dough. Somebody ate an expensive Christmas cookie that year. It was family tradition to go to New York City on Christmas Eve and see the sights, have dinner, shop, and then take a carriage ride through Central Park. At dinner, which was in the Theater District, I told the waiter to delay dinner. In front of my children and about 50 patrons, I got down on one knee and pulled out her engagement ring and asked her if she would marry me again? Lori stood up, and I stood up. I took her hand and placed the ring on her finger. Then, I put my hands around her waist and she put her arms around my shoulder, and she said, "Yes." Just like old times. We gave each other a little kiss and everybody clapped. She asked me, "How?" I said, "Don't worry, no need to explain." We sat down to eat, and gave my usual toast to good health and family for the next year. All through dinner, Lori kept telling me she was sorry for losing the diamond. I told her not to worry about it. We got home that night, opened presents at around 1:00 AM, and said goodnight to the kids. We closed our bedroom door. She turned to me, jumped on me and said, "Now you know you were the one!" Just like the day I asked her to marry me on Good Friday in '83. It brought tears to my eyes, the memories of a day gone by. To rekindle our love so long ago, to know our love for each other has never died, it only got stronger.

THE WORD NOBODY WANTS TO HEAR

It was around February 5, 2012. Lori called me at work. She said we got an invitation to a Valentine's Day ball in Atlantic City and she wanted to go. Could I get a room for the night? Sure I told her, I also told her to go out and get a dress.

See a couple years ago, Lori and I were at home. I was working on my boat. Lori was in the garden. She asked me if I wanted to take her for a ride? I said, sure. We cleaned up; I already knew where she wanted to go to, down to Atlantic City. We arrived at our casino, went inside to get something to eat, and then went to gamble. She was playing at her machine; I was just walking around looking at the new machines. I sat down at one machine, put in 20 bucks, pressed the button and watched the reels go around. Nothing was coming up. When I hit the button again the bonus game came out. I had to pick five boxes totaling 55 or more. If that happened I won the jackpot. I picked the boxes straight across the bottom row and in each of those boxes the number 11 came out, so I had a total of 55. I won the jackpot! The bells started ringing, the machine locked up. All I saw were people gathering around me saying, you won the jackpot! Ok, I did.

Lori came running. She said, "You won!" I said, "I won!" I didn't know how much though until security came and told us. Five figures. I never heard Lori scream so loud, I think I was in shock. Lori took full advantage of the situation though. She asked for a glass of champagne. Security took me in the back room and asked me how I wanted my money? I said in ones, Lori hit me on the head. I said I'll take 5,000 in cash and to give me a check for the rest; I split the money with Lori. The check went into the bank that night. They gave us a dinner for two. The bill totaled $785 with two bottles of champagne, good thing I didn't have to pay for that. They also gave us a room, fit for king and his queen. I was still in shock, Lori was soaking it in. The room was as big as a house. There was a pool in the middle of the room. "Do you believe this?" I said to myself. The hosts for the hotel left us alone, and as the double doors closed behind us, they said if you need anything just call and your butler will get it for you. The clothes came off; Lori went into the pool with bath salts. I was still in shock, "Look at this room" I said,

"Where's the TV?" Lori said, "Forget about the TV, close the lights and come in."

There we were, just the two of us again with a bottle of champagne in such a romantic situation and all it cost me was a $20.00 bill. It was beautiful. Just Lori and I, words were exchanged, whispering in each other's ear, kisses and hugs, our usual thing. It was just the right setting. We got out of the pool and, as usual, we didn't even dry ourselves off before we went to bed.

So ever since the day that I won that money I guess the casino thought I was a high roller and kept sending me freebies through the mail. Lori and I went to the Valentine's Day ball, myself in a suit. Lori, at 49, was gorgeous looking to me. Everything about her just fell into place. She had a blue dress just above the knees, her shoulders slightly exposed, and high heels. That's my wife, she is beautiful. I am the luckiest husband alive. We danced, ate, and drank; it was a beautiful night out together. Towards the end of the night, Lori asked me to get her some anti-acid pills. "What for?" I asked. She said, "It's probably just something I ate." The following day we went home. Lori still had a little indigestion for the next couple of days, but then it went away.

During the next couple of weeks I noticed Lori looking a little weak and gaunt. She explained to me she has been getting bad cases of acid reflux from time to time. I told her it was time to see a doctor. This was around June of 2012. Lori finally sought medical help and her doctor issued her a prescription. It seemed to work for a while, but then the acid reflux came back. She was very frustrated and tired of the constant, burning pain. A few weeks later, she went back to the doctors and he expressed his concern to her, scheduling an endoscopy in July of 2012. In the meantime, we took the kids camping in Pennsylvania and had a great time together as a family. However, the kids started to notice that their mother wasn't looking well and wasn't eating much. Lori and I explained to them that we were taking care of the situation and not to worry. It's not like we wanted to lie to our kids or keep them in the dark, but when you're a parent you want to protect your children and keep them from worrying. Truthfully, we weren't entirely sure what was going on yet.

In July, Lori traveled to the hospital with her mother for the endoscopy; it was an in-and-out procedure. About a week later, I received a call from Lori and she was crying hysterically. "What, honey?" I asked. "The doctor's office called...they want me to come in and bring somebody with me. Oh honey, I'm so scared." I tried to comfort her the best I could over the phone. I told her I would be on my way home immediately. It usually only took me about forty-five minutes to get home from work, but this time it seemed like hours. While driving, I made a call to the doctor's office. The office manager answered and put me in touch with the doctor directly. "I need to know what my wife has before I see her, so I can be strong for her. Please tell me." And the doctor said the most terrifying, upsetting set of words that one never wants to hear. "Steve, Lori has stage three stomach cancer." The world stopped at that moment. In a trance, I was able to thank the doctor for telling me and that I would see him in a couple hours with Lori. As I hung up the phone, I began to stare at the road in front of me. Filled with anger and sadness, I called my mother-in-law and ordered her to rush down to our house immediately. "Lori needs your support. I need your support. I just spoke to the doctor. She has stomach cancer."

Once I arrived home, I couldn't bring myself to get out of the car. My whole world was crumbling down. I began to continuously slam my fist into the steering wheel with anger. I cried so much my eyes swelled up. How could this happen to her, to us, to my family? She never did anything wrong in this world. Why is she being punished? "Punish me, not her!" I yelled out loud. I had to clean myself up before I went inside; I had to be strong for Lori. We will prevail. As I walked inside I observed Lori laying down, watching television. I walked over to her, bent down towards her with my arms open, and I embraced her. She hugged me with all her might. "I knew it!" she exclaimed. "You knew what, honey?" I replied back. "It's probably cancer!" Lori stated. "If it is, we will fight this, and take care of it; we will fight this together, sweetheart." I pulled her up off the couch, grabbed her purse and off we were to the doctors. We arrived at the office promptly. Lori sat on the gurney, her mother sat on the chair, and I stood in the doorway. The doctor came into the room. He had a sad look to his face but with a smile. Lori said, "What do I have?" He said, "You have stomach cancer." I held my composure as Lori's mom sat still. Then, Lori slammed her hand down on the table and said, "Ok, where do we start?" I said to myself, *what a woman I have, so strong, and so determined to beat this disease.* She didn't even cry. The doctor told us we would have to find a surgeon. We said okay. We said our goodbyes and thanked him; that's where the fight started.

Lori told her mother, thank god it wasn't the kids, or Steven, because she couldn't have handled it. Now I started to cry. She said to stop with the waterworks. I told her over and over again, "Honey, I love you." "I know sweetheart, I know" she said. I told her that she and I would fight this like we've fought throughout our lives, together as one, "I feel, you feel." As I said this, Lori replied, "I know you will take care of me, Steven." *There was not a doubt in my mind that I would.*

We didn't tell the kids yet. That night her mom and dad went home, it was only Lori and I. We went to bed and we talked, not about what could happen, but about the first time we met and how she knew that I was chosen for her. I said "Who told you?" and she said "God did." She knew from the start that I was the one she was to marry, she even told her cousin Paula when they were in Sicily back in the summer of '78. Paula told me years later about it. Lori said in her love letters to me that if she ever got sick that I was the only one to take care of her. I knew that I was not only Lori's husband, but that I was her caregiver. We fell asleep embraced in each other's arms.

The next morning, Lori called her friend that she worked with; she gave us her friend's name who worked with a cancer center in Pennsylvania. She gave us the name of the surgeon in PA. We called to make an appointment. We met the doctor that Wednesday. He opened the door and was smiling. "Hello, to both of you," he said. He examined Lori and took a look at the scans. I asked all the questions. He said he would do the surgery on Saturday, which was three days away. We were ok with that.

"What a doctor!" Lori said, "He makes me feel comfortable." "That's what you want," I told her. She also stated a few times that he was her guardian angel. "Whatever you want honey," I told her. Now, Lori and I had insurance, but it was a new insurance policy and the doctor knew that. He said we might have a problem, so he would call us on Friday. Friday came. Lori and I went out for a late lunch. The doctor called and said, "Lori, I want you to go to the emergency room tonight. I'll have somebody admit you and you will be good to go on Saturday morning." So that's what we did. I got her a private room so that I could stay there with her the whole night. Morning came, she slept the whole night. I wish I knew what was going through her mind. Of course, I was up all night pacing the halls, sitting by her side, holding her hand and asking myself, why? I had no answer. I felt emptiness inside my soul. The nurses came in and prepped Lori. I walked beside her as they pushed the bed towards the operating rooms. Before she went through the double doors of no admittance, the staff said, "It's ok for you to give her a kiss." So I bent down to give her a kiss, still holding her hand, and I said, "I love you." She said, "I love you too honey, don't leave me!" I said, "Don't you leave me!" We slowly let go of each other's hands, she blew me a kiss, and at that moment the doors closed shut. My emotions took control of me. I finally broke down, "Was that it, was that my last goodbye?", I said to myself. I went to the waiting room where all the family members were waiting. I couldn't even get ahold of my emotions there. I had to be comforted, I wanted to take my wife's pain away and give it to myself. The operation only took two and a half hours to complete. The staff kept me posted from start to finish. The hospital staff was so compassionate. They made us feel comfortable and relaxed, saying everything's going to be ok, she's doing fine.

Finally, she was out; they put her in a private room in ICU. She had tubes coming out of her entire body. I asked questions nonstop. I needed to know answers, because that's my wife. She came out of recovery; she was ok but in a lot of pain. I was the first one into the room. "Honey," I said. "Sweetie!" she replied to me. "I love you." "I love you too." The kids went in, and then everybody else.

I took off from work the whole week she was in the hospital. I was allowed to sleep in her room the entire time, take a shower and shave. Thank God. Three days later, she was out of ICU and into a regular room. I didn't sleep much. Lori was looking good and improving. What's the saying, I sleep with one eye open and one eye shut? This is my soul mate since I was 14. If you didn't treat my wife right, you'd hear it from me. Lori was eating now, but not as much. Things were still healing and she didn't have a stomach anymore, it was a big adjustment for both of us. One morning, I was sitting on the bed with Lori and one of the doctors, or should I say interns, came into the room with a group of students. He started to say to them, "In this case…" Before he could say anything else, my wife stopped him in his tracks. She said, "I'm not a case. I have a name, and my name is Lori Zarycki and this is my husband Steven!" Well, that intern turned red like a tomato. I guess that's what they're taught to do instead of going by first names. My wife remembered that saying from the movie Patch Adams, smart woman my wife was. During our stay in the hospital, I did a lot of research on her type of cancer. I made a lot of calls to different organizations to seek information for myself as a caregiver, to prepare myself for down the road. It was August 15, 2012, Lori's 50th birthday, and she was going home. She couldn't wait to leave. The only thing that bothered her was a feeding tube in her belly. It was there just for extra nutrients, that I would have to give her twice a day by machine. She dressed herself, I packed the bags, gathered all the flowers, and we left the hospital. On the way home, all we were doing was talking and talking, about everything. I guess we were just glad to be in each other's company, or we were nervous about the future.

We arrived home. The whole family was there. There was also a cake for my wife. What a milestone, turning 50. She really looked great, although she said it sucked with all the stiches down her belly, and the feeding tube going to go soon. Lori was a tough cookie. Some days went by, she was getting stronger. A big adjustment for her though was only eating about a handful of food at a time, or only drinking a cup of tea or coffee. Her intestines were doing three jobs now instead of two: holding, breaking down, and waste. My poor baby. If I could've switched places with her I would, because she didn't deserve this. Believe it or not, Lori went back to work three weeks later. *I know, are you kidding me?* She was getting annoyed about the feeding tube. It was at a spot on her waist where she couldn't button her pants. I had to clean it every day and hook her up at night for about an hour to give her nutrients, but she was eating regularly. So, Lori called the doctor to ask if the feeding tube could be removed. He said, sure. So one day at work, the doctor in her office building came to her work place and pulled it out. That's all it took, she was happy. In the following months a very dear friend of mine, named Sue, called me and asked if she could help the family. She was somebody I could rest my head on and cry. She knew what troubles we were having with the insurance, having to pay all the bills out of pocket. So what she did was organize an auction for my wife. They named it the Love for Lori Gift Auction. Sue donated so much of her own time. Hundreds of people showed up, donating money, gifts, and all sorts of things. I am deeply grateful for what Sue did for my wife and our family. I appealed against the insurance company on behalf of my wife and lost due to, what they said was, a pre-existing condition. Are you kidding me?! *It's unbelievable how a panel of experts can say who's to live or who's to die. Sometimes it gets to be how the world works. I guess that's just the way it is though, unfortunately.*

THE ROAD TO RECOVERY

Our next journey was to chemo and radiation. We were not looking forward to it. But, Lori had such a strong personality and that kept her marching on. We met the oncologist. He told Lori she would have to do chemo at least once a month and radiation once a week. *What a life changing experience for both of us.* One thing that bothered Lori a lot was losing her hair. That beautiful hair of hers, which was Lori. The doctor said it wouldn't fall out, but that it would be very dry and brittle. She was ok with that. I told her, "you lose your hair, your son and I will lose ours!" She cried. I hugged her; she gave me a kiss and said, "Thank you, honey." Weeks were going by, it was almost Halloween. I was in high gear every day, making sure she did what she had to do. She worried about me a lot. I told her, "Don't you know me by now? I'm ok. I'm here by your side."

The storm of all storms hits the Jersey Shore, Hurricane Sandy. We were hit badly; we had four feet of water in our house, no electricity for eleven days. I sat down on the stairs in the backyard after the storm, overlooking the devastation the water caused. I put my head between my legs, my hands crossed around my neck and I started to cry. I asked again, why! Next thing, Lori came outside and sat next to me. She put her arm around my shoulder and gave me a kiss on the cheek. "Don't worry my love," she said. "We've been through a lot together in our lifetime. Together we've climbed stairs and been pushed back. But we keep going. We faced obstacles and jumped hurdles. We will get through this, I love you," she said.

Our son Chris took charge. He assembled all his friends together, bought two dumpsters, and cleaned it all. Of course I helped a little, but I was tired, we got through it. Lori and I kept going through the routine of chemo and radiation month after month up until December. We went to the doctor's office; she got her blood work done that morning. He then came in and told us there was no more need for chemotherapy or radiation for a while. Lori's eyes filled up with tears. I held my emotions for her. I wanted her to breathe and cherish what the doctor had just said. She gave the doctor a hug; I got a bigger hug, of course. Lori asked the doctor if it was ok to go on vacation. "Sure, why not?" he said. "When you get back, we will schedule you for a CAT scan in April or May. But for now, you go and enjoy yourself." Lori was so happy when we got into the car. I sat in the driver's seat; Lori got out of her seat and sat down on my lap while I was driving. Talk about dangerous. We used to do that a lot back in the day when we didn't have to wear seat belts, and we did it at night when nobody could see. She put her head on my shoulder and started kissing my neck and my ears. She started breathing heavy into my ears, the car was going faster. I said to her, "We're going to get into an accident." She said that if she died, at least she would die in my arms and with the one she loved. We got home safely. She made dinner, nobody was home. The kids had gone out, so we went to bed early and relaxed. I asked Lori where she wanted to go on vacation. "Jamaica," she said. "Okay," I said. Meanwhile, the weekend was coming and the kids had gotten tickets to a concert in Atlantic City for one of our favorite bands growing up, Boston. I couldn't wait, neither could Lori. Lori asked me if I could get a room. I said, ok. I called up the hotel and said, I needed a room for a special occasion. They gave me a suite. The kids loved it but they were not going to stay for the weekend. The tub in the room had stairs to get into it. The room had two bedrooms, a bar, and a master suite with a canopy bed. Right up my wife's alley. The concert was great, it brought back memories. The kids went home and Lori and I stayed.

It was a night to remember. Lori was in remission and she couldn't have been happier. She whispered to me, "Thank you for caring for me." "That's my job, Sweetie. Remember, till death do us part." I quoted from a movie, "Remember, honey. You jump, I jump. That's how it's been all our lives, and I'm not going to leave your side. I never have and never will." I asked Lori, "You remember when you told me I was the one?" "Of course," she said. "Well, am I still the one?" "Always and forever till the day I die." Lori walked down the stairs into the tub to relax. She said, "Are you going to stare at me all night?" "Maybe," I said. "Or are you going to come in and wash my back?", Lori asked. Could I resist? Not this time. The following morning she was on the Internet looking for resorts in Jamaica. She found the resort she wanted in Ocho Rios and booked it.

The second week in March, we left for Jamaica for nine days. It was first class all the way from the airplane to the limo to the hotel. It was a vacation well deserved for Lori and I. It was nice driving up the coast in a limo to the resort. The driver stopped along the way to show us some of the history of the island, he also picked us up some tropical drinks. We arrived at the resort and were treated like royalty. We were showed to our suite and fell in love again. Lori wasted no time putting on her bikini and her body wrap. She was looking hot. As for me, I gained a little weight. I was ok with the weight gain. She knew that it was due to all the worrying I was doing; I was eating a lot at night, that's when I put the weight on. We went straight to the beach and got our drinks. I carried her into the water and it was warm like bath water. She put her arms around my neck and I began to bob up and down. She put her head on my shoulders and closed her eyes. Lori deserved this, *she even got her hair wet and she didn't care.*

We went back to the lounge chairs and relaxed. Lori had our stay at the resort already planned out for the week. Everything expect the nights, they just seemed to fall into place like they always have with us. Dinner, dancing, shows, the casino, walking barefoot on the beach, and our alone time. I surprised her one evening with a couple's massage on the beach. She held my hand tightly, both of us looking at one another while we were lying down on separate tables. She had tears in her eyes. "What's the matter, honey?" I said. "Nothing, sweetheart." Lori told me, "I'm just happy and in love and glad to be here with you." After an hour massage, I was like melted butter. We went back to the room and got ready for another night of romance, dinner, and dancing. The next morning after breakfast, Lori had an excursion all planned out. We were going to climb the falls at Dunn's River. She wanted to get a videotape of the entire day, so I had to find somebody to do that. Then we went to a Jamaican style barbecue, and late for a speed boat ride along the island. I said to Lori, "Hey, girl. You trying to kill me or something?" *It was all good, I just got a little winded at times. I enjoyed it though.* It was like she found the fountain of youth, but after a whole day of non-stop adventure we were exhausted. We got back to the resort all sunburned, got a drink and relaxed, The next day was spent on the beach, tanning. Lori said I looked like one of the islanders there because I tan quickly, and we were only there for four days so far.

Lori was fond of animals throughout her life, so I tried finding some kind of game farm or petting zoo. Instead I found something Lori only dreamed about, and that was riding horses on the beach. I surprised her the next day. We went to a horse ranch. We had a private guide that took us through the mountains, sugar cane fields, and then to our own beach where they had a picnic setup for us; drinks and Jamaican-style food, it was perfect. We dismounted our horses, laid down on beach mats, ate lunch, and drank some rum punch. I think I drank a little too much though, because the horse I was riding the first time seemed to be larger the second time. Now it was time to ride the horses on the beach. There were no saddles on the horses or reins to hold onto. I said to Lori, "Are you kidding me?" She laughed and said, "Watch me!" Lori rode horses, and quite well. For me, well, that's a whole different story. I wasn't watching and Lori was already on the horse, the guide telling her, "You go, girl." She was off and running. I started to tear up as I saw her ride off. The guide asked me, "What's the matter, man?" I told him what she went through. He told me, "She'll be ok, man. Enjoy life!" I said to him, "You know, if this is cancer and this is how she's handling it, I know that she's going to be ok." Now it was my turn. I got on the horse and held on for dear life. I caught up with Lori and then it was just her and I at a slow gallop at the water's edge. The sun was beating down on us, but the horse's hooves were kicking the water into our faces. What a way to cool off. It was so romantic for us. One of Lori's fantasies that came true. I was so happy that I could honor her by giving her this gift. We rode for about 45 minutes, sometimes just walking the horses slowly, or other times at full gallop. *What an experience we had.* We rode back to our resort, got a drink or two, and then it was back to our room. The rest of the week went fantastic for both of us, lying out on the sand, soaking up the sun, dinner, dancing and, of course, romancing. What a great trip we had. Lori said that in another two years we would plan a trip to Antigua to renew our vows, for our 30 year anniversary.

Stairways

Steven Zarycki

A SLAP IN THE FACE

We arrived back home safely from our vacation and life was just peachy. We both went back to work, like normal. However, we had to make an appointment now for her P.E.T. scan. She wasn't looking forward to it and neither was I, but it was something we had to do. She had done the scan before, and now we waited on pins and needles for the next appointment. A week later we found out the results. She got her blood work done like the normal procedure and then the doctor came in. He said it was all good. I asked him twice, "Is she cancer free?" He said "Yes, but…" "But what?" I said. He responded by telling us there was a spot the size of a lemon down by her female organs. "What is it?" Lori asked. "I don't know. You're going to have to go to your gynecologist and get it checked out." Lori was in shock. "Are you kidding me?" Lori proclaimed. We then said thank you and left.

Lori and I talked after leaving the office and decided to find a new oncologist. A couple of days later we were in the hospital because Lori was having really bad belly pains. It seems fluid was building up inside and it had to be drained. While she was in the hospital, the doctors did a biopsy on that lemon-sized spot.

When we returned home Lori was tired. So she put on the TV and laid down. I went outside, lit a fire and sat down, gazing into the flames. I sat there saying my prayers, telling whoever wanted to listen to please tell me this was just a dream. This isn't going to happen twice, not to my wife, not to our family. Let me have cancer instead of her. She never did anything wrong! Why, I said. Why, why, why!

nobody answered me.

I wiped away my tears and walked up the stairs into the house. Lori was lying down on her lounge chair, the TV was on, and she was now looking at a magazine. I laid down next to her and put my arm under her back, just holding her. She started giving me kisses on my forehead telling me she loved me and that it was going to be all right. "You didn't have to go outside and cry," she told me. "You were spying on me?", I said. She always had a way of doing that. "You could've cried inside," she said. Lori reassured me again that things were going to be all right. My adrenaline kicked in. My level of anxiety was running out of control and it seemed as if it wasn't going to stop.

A week later, we were back at the doctor's. It seemed like déjà vu. He walked in and he said, "Your cancer came back." What a slap in the face for Lori and I. "You told us two weeks ago she was cancer free!" I said. *"What is going on?"* Lori yelled. We were pissed off at this doctor. Lori said, "Let's go!" We left, went home and made a call to our friend at the hospital in Pennsylvania to get a good gynecologist. We made an appointment and in two days we went to Philadelphia with test results in hand. We met with her new doctor, a nice woman, compassionate and head of her department. Lori got a check-up and, thank God, no ovarian cancer. We told the doctor that the other doctor we previously worked with in N.J. and how they said the tumor was the size of a lemon and that she was cancer free at that time. The doctor then looked at us with a puzzled look. It seemed like she was confused on who this other doctor was and if he even knew what he was talking about. "Well, Lori, we have to take it out," she said. "Take it all out. I'm not going to have any more kids at this age," Lori replied. So we scheduled an appointment.

While at the office, we set up for a new operation in two weeks. She was nervous, I was a basket case. I couldn't show her, I had to be strong. It was Friday already and we left for the hospital. We arrived there early, around 6am. She was scheduled for 8 a.m. They did blood work on Lori; her white blood cell count was down. You need them to fight off infection, so it was a two hour delay until her blood got to the correct level. Lori was pissed off, but what can you do. Finally everything was good to go. I gave her a big kiss and a hug, and she did the same back to me. She said that she was sorry for putting me through this. I said, "Are you kidding me? I jump, you jump. Do you remember?!" "Yes," Lori said with a laugh. I told her I would see her in two hours. *The hospital was backed up with operations so Lori was late coming out of surgery.*

I went to the waiting room, my mother-in-law was there. Just seeing her made me racked with emotions. She came over to me, gave me a hug, and told me to relax. I said to her, "Why us? Why Lori? It's not fair." "Your right. Life isn't fair," she said. Two hours seem like four hours. Finally, Lori came out of surgery. The doctor came to speak with me in the waiting room. She said everything went well and that Lori was ok. "But Steve," she said, "that tumor was the size of a football. I don't know why the doctor told you it was small?" "I don't either," I said. I thanked the doctor and went to see Lori in the recovery room with my mother-in-law. Lori looked really good and this time she didn't have a lot of tubes coming out of her like the first time, just an IV for pain medication. I bent down over the railing and gave her a kiss. She smiled at me and said I love you. I said I love you back. Then she told me she wasn't doing this ever again and she meant it. She only spent two days in the hospital. I stayed at the hotel down the street. I didn't want to leave her side but she had another woman in her room so I was not allowed to stay overnight. We went home three days later. Lori actually wanted to go home in two days and the doctor said no, so of course Lori was mad. We made a new appointment with a new oncologist at the cancer center in Pennsylvania for the following weeks. It wasn't something we were looking forward to, but it was something we had to get done.

It was our time again. Lori didn't have to go back to work yet. She needed time to heal. I went back to work; I needed to get my mind clear. Lori was a great cook, actually a gourmet cook. I always told her she could take a stick of butter and make it taste 100 different ways. She kept busy. She drove herself to wherever she needed to go, usually to pamper herself or to shop. I usually called her three times a day just to check up on her. *That's the way I was, I loved her.*

The weekend came and Lori wanted to go out. So we went out to a craft fair at a local state forest. Lori wasn't into crafts too much, but they had other things to do there. After about 2 hours of walking, she wanted to go shopping. So we went to the store. She felt a little dizzy, so I got her a carriage to lean on. All of a sudden she yells out, "Steven!", started shaking and then she fell to the ground. Good thing I was there and caught her. I laid her down on the ground. "Call 911," I said to the manager. I put her head sideways, so she wouldn't choke, and opened her airway. The manager got me a wet towel, she was coming to. The ambulance came. I told the paramedics her medical condition, that she was anemic, and usually her iron was low. We went to the local hospital and they gave her fluids and did blood work. Sure enough, she was dehydrated and had low iron. I had never experienced that before, but somehow I was prepared. *That's what caregivers are there for*. We left the hospital and about three hours later she wanted to go eat barbecue that night, of all things. I said to her, "Haven't you had enough for one day?" "Please," she said to me with those puppy dog eyes. She reached over to me in the car and started kissing me on my neck. "Ok." I said. But deep in the back of my mind, I was on high alert. I called her mom and made Lori talk to her to tell her what went on. You know, Lori didn't want any help from anybody else but me. I was her caregiver, husband, and driver. I don't know what else I was, and I didn't care, because she was my wife and I would do anything for her. Even if I was burning myself out, she came first. We had dinner and went home. I was exhausted, so I went to bed early at around 10:00 PM. The TV was on, the lights were off. She stepped out of the bath tub smelling like lavender. Lori snuggled into bed naked. She said she was sorry. I said, "For what now? It was an exciting day." "Well, you know", she said. "Oh stop!" I said. "What do you want me to do, run away and leave you? You're my wife, I'll do anything I have to for you." She put her leg over my body and said, "I love you, honey." "Well I guess you do, don't you" I said. We had a romantic night, but it was gentle. It brought back memories of the times gone by, when we were first dating. Through the years it never changed. We were still passionate, romantic, and a little silly at times, but it never left us and I hope it never will.

We had about two weeks before her first appointment, so the following weekend she wanted to go for a ride. We headed west. As I was driving, I told her I was bored. She said to me, "You want to go?" "Go where?", I said. "Let's go upstate to the cabin." "You don't have to ask me twice." I made a right hand turn and started north. We had only the clothes on our backs. On the way up the New York State Thruway, she said to me to look for a drugstore and a clothing store to get some supplies. *Easy for her to say, I was doing all the driving.*

Lori called up to see if the cabin was available, unfortunately they were closed for the season. It was around the end of October 2013, most of the places usually close around this time up there because of the early snow. We weren't discouraged, she found another place. Lori told the proprietors we'd be there around 10:00 PM. They said they would leave the key under the mat at cabin Number One. Lori asked about firewood. They said, no problem, it would be in the cabin. We were set, all we had to do was to get there.

We finally arrived around 11:00 p.m. It was dark and secluded in the woods, right up our ally. It was raining that night, leaves were still falling and it was cold outside. We walked into the cabin, well, I carried her in. She gave me a kiss and went right to work starting a fire. It was a big cabin, two bedrooms, kitchen, open family room with the queen size bed near the fireplace, so guess where we slept. It was nice, but not as cozy as our usual place. We made the most of our weekend getaways, always romantic and passionate, and found things to do. She somehow knew when the fire was going out during the night. She would always nudge me to put more logs on the fire to keep it going, then she would hug me and kiss me all night. No sleep of course, but that was Lori and I for 28 years of marriage. You know what I thought, that this was a great time this weekend to celebrate 28 years of marriage. The past July she was in a hospital, so we didn't celebrate.

So I asked her what she wanted to do in the morning, even though it was the morning already. "Let's go to Vermont," she said. So we fell asleep for about 3 hours, got up, dressed and off we went. It was a beautiful day, the sun was shining, no clouds in the sky. It was cool outside but it warmed up eventually, the leaves still had their color. A typical New England fall day. We took the ferry across Lake Champlain into Burlington, Vermont. We went to farms, apple orchards, local bazaars, and general stores. Lori and I used to take the kids up here when they were younger, so we knew the area very well. It was a great day for her and I, just relaxing, because we knew when we got back we were going to have to start the doctor rounds again. I was relaxed, but I was always on guard. I surprised her again; I told her we were having dinner at seven. "For what?" she said. I said, "Our 28th wedding anniversary." "How romantic," she said.

We got back to the cabin around 6:30 p.m., freshened up a little and went to the restaurant. It was a fancy place for where it was, a closely guarded secret for the locals. Lori ordered prime rib and I had the same. We ate, had a drink and took a doggie bag back with us to the cabin. The embers were still red from the morning. Lori told me to start the fire, which was a first. "Were you going?" I asked her. With a typical Lori flirty voice, "I'm going to put something comfortable on." I got the fire started and 20 minutes had passed. What the hell is taking her so long?, I said to myself. I tiptoed to the bathroom, but she heard me coming because the floor was uneven. "I'll be right out!" she said. I smelled the curling iron; I wondered what the hell she is doing in there. Finally, the door slowly opened. Wow, I got all choked up. Words couldn't come out of my mouth. I was stunned with the overall beauty of my wife. That she would do this for me, what a woman. Even at 51, she looked as beautiful as she did back when we first met. Everything was perfect from her hair to her toes. She had my white collard work shirt on. I always wondered why I didn't have enough work shirts for the office. My wife could stop the rain if it was raining outside. Lori walked over to me with flirty movements. I grabbed her waist and she put her arms around my neck. "Happy Anniversary, my love!" she said in a low tone. "I love you". "I love you, too." Then a blast from the past came out of me, "Do you wanna?" I was like a kid again. Lori started to tear up, so I wiped her mascara from her cheek. She said, "You remembered?" "How could I forget?", I said. She nodded her head. I swept her off her feet and laid her in bed. What a beautiful way to celebrate 28 years of marriage and many more anniversaries to come. I was just at a loss of words thinking, she just keeps going on enjoying life, and I do love her so...

 I woke up early that morning and sat down on the railing on the porch with a cup of coffee. I watched the sun rise over the mountains and the sunbeams peering down between the trees. I was in deep mediation thinking 'what if?' They were bad thoughts…I had to be positive. I have to be strong for her, not to let her know I was breaking down inside. Not only in my heart, but my wellbeing. Just inside the cabin lies my soul mate dreaming of a night she just spent with her husband. I can't spoil it for her, she's fighting a battle within herself, she wants to win this battle, not only for herself but for her children and for me. I know she has, in the back of her mind, thoughts about the worst and what would happen to me if she died. We talked about it a couple of months back. I told her back then, "I will do my best not to let it happen, and it's not going to, so stop." She kept on insisting she knew what was going to happen and told me what she wanted me to do. I said "Ok, enough." I heard footsteps from inside the cabin, Lori was awake. She peered out the window at me, smiled and blew me a kiss. Boy, she even looked beautiful in the morning, she always did. God created this woman for me. I thank you, Lord.

She opened the door. "Morning, honey," she said to me in a soft voice. "Ok," I said, "I'll get you coffee, you get dressed." We didn't want to go home but we had to. After breakfast, we went to one of the historic forts in town to take pictures of the lake. It was a sunny day that morning, but the lake had a mist rising from its cold waters. Lori was in one of her playful moods. She said, "Come on, slow poke. Time to climb twenty eight stairs." "For what?" I said. "For 28 years of marriage," Lori said. So we started to climb. After we reached the twenty eighth stair, she wanted loose change. I only had two quarters in my pocket. "What do you need them for?" I asked. "Dig a small hole by this sapling, put the two quarters in the hole and cover them up." "For what?" I said, again. So next time we come up here and I need money for coffee I know where to look. I thought it was funny but odd. Or was there a real reason she made me do that? Then we headed home. It was a five hour trip back. It was starting to rain and it was gloomy out. Lori still had a smile on and that was good; we both knew what was coming up this following week at the doctor's.

Wednesday was here already; we were both nervous. We arrived at the chemo center, a beautiful building in the historic part of Philadelphia. Lori had her blood taken, I did the paperwork, and we waited for the doctor. He came in with a smile and greeted Lori and I. He explained what type of chemo Lori would be getting and some of the after affects. The treatment would take about two and a half hours each visit. The doctor said Lori's cancer was gastric carcinoma, one of the heavy hitters, but he told us it could be controlled. At least this doctor didn't pull punches, he told us what we were up against. The staff called the doctor a 'walking medical journal', he was also the head of the department. Lori was very comfortable and relaxed with him, that's what she needed.

The nurses started the procedure, I felt so helpless. I felt her pain when the nurses placed the needle in her arm. If they didn't get the needle in right the first time they had to do it again, it was so traumatizing for Lori. I didn't want to see her go through this again, but she had to. The doctor also told her that her hair would start falling out in two weeks. That's all she needed to hear. Lori's eyes started to glass over as she looked at me. I was so at a loss of words. Again, I told her, "You lose your hair, I will lose mine. You jump, I jump. Remember?" "That's not necessary," Lori said to me. She said she would just cut her hair short so it wouldn't be so traumatic for her. Then Lori asked me, "You'll take me shopping for wigs honey, won't you?" "Of course, I will", I said. The doctor also told her that she could go on disability because the chemo will make her tired and a little sick to her abdomen. Lori smiled and said, "Well, I deserve it. I've been working a long time. I need a break."

We went home. She was tired, but she still made dinner, watched TV, clipped coupons and played games on her iPhone. I cleaned the house and sat next to her after I was done. I put my arm around her and gave her a kiss on the head; I told her I was going to be ok. She said, "I know you're lying, but can we go shopping for wigs tomorrow after work?" I said, "Of course, honey." Lori went to work the following day and gave her boss the disability papers. He wasn't a happy person, but it's not her fault she got sick. This is what had to be done. After 20 years of working for him as an office manager it was tough for both of them. Lori was kind of glad though, she deserved the rest. A week later she parted with the office. She left behind a great friend, her name was Lori as well, but they still kept in touch.

Lori was home now. Her next visit to the doctor was next month, so we went shopping for wigs. I didn't realize how many styles there were. I was joking with her about a pink and blond wig I saw. I said, "Can you wear this one when you go to bed at night?" She said, "Sure, just get me high heels and a garter belt." We both started laughing, and that was good, at least she still had a sense of humor. Then Lori tried on a 1980s style wig and that's all it took to get my emotions rolling. She said, "I'm sorry!" "For what now!", I said. "Because I picked up this wig. I understood that it would bring back memories of us." So she put the wig back and picked up two or three that were the normal style now. She looked great with anything she put on. Lori said, "I don't have to wash or style the wigs, so we can be out of the house faster." I knew that she would miss doing her hair and that bothered her, but she was strong. It had been a couple of months now and Lori was tolerating the chemo very well. The doctors said everything was looking ok, not great, but just ok.

Christmas time was finally here again. Lori was baking cookies, as usual. Alexis was home from school again, helping her mother with the cooking and shopping.

Chris now had a girlfriend, her name was Shelby. She was a sweet girl. Lori and I loved her and always will. She was just right for Chris. Blond, blue-eyed, she wasn't as tall as Lori, but she kept Chris in his place. That year, it actually snowed during the carriage ride. I'll never forget Lori crying because she was so happy it snowed.

After a whole day of walking and shopping, we left New York, went home, and unwrapped gifts. The kids did pretty well that year with gifts. I gave Lori a ring, a very special ring just for her. A ring that showed my unconditional love for her, a ring for strength and courage, a ring telling her I will be by her side in sickness and in health, no matter what life held for us in the future, I will always and forever be there for her.

That night, we closed our bedroom doors. It was quite in the house. Lori and I shared our thoughts together, bad ones and good ones. We realized through our life together that talking was the best medicine in a relationship; it kept us strong and in love for 40 years. It's a new year, 2014, and Lori has been going through chemo every month now. Back and forth we went to Pennsylvania. Usually we had to go back a week later because she would dehydrate or need some other medicine to stabilize her blood. It became almost routine. Lori was always thin and chemo, unfortunately, made her even thinner. I would pace the halls in the hospital just wanting to talk to somebody instead of myself and ask them, "Why!?" *Why is she going through this?* I just needed somebody to listen.

RECOVERY: ROUND TWO

One day, after arriving at the chemo center, I told Lori to sit in a wheelchair and I would push her around. "Why walk?" I said. So she did and I was wheeling her down the hall. Lori was looking out the window at the park to her right. I was coming up to the chemo lab and I stopped and glanced to my left. Lori was still looking out the window. I noticed a young girl. I would say she was around nineteen years old. She was there in the room with her mother, a doctor, and two nurses. She was a cute girl. She had no hair, just a headband and too little earrings on. She was hooked up to a chemotherapy machine, it was sad. I nudged Lori, she looked up at me, and I motioned to her to look to the left. What Lori did next didn't surprise me, but it surprised the people around that young girl. Lori put out her hand to touch this girl, and said, "Lord, give this girl my life so she can experience the love I had. I lived the good life, give her a chance." Talk about an ocean of tears, I don't think there was a dry eye in the house. For Lori to say what she did showed me who my wife really was deep inside, she was a woman filled with so much love, that she would give her own life to a perfect stranger. I love her so.

It was around February when Lori got a letter saying she was getting a respite vacation for two in Florida with all expenses paid. She called me at work, to tell me the good news. I said, "Really, honey? That's great news! When are we supposed to go?" "Next week, sweetheart," she said. "All right, I have to see if I can take off from work." I really didn't see any problem in it. My boss at the time, his name was Anthony, was really understanding of what we were both going through. He was by my side for the whole time. He was truly a brother to me, and he knew what our family was dealing with. He gave me as much time as I needed to take care of her and my family. People like him really supported me to push through.

So are bags were packed. We took off on one of the coldest days ever, the plane was even having trouble starting. Eventually, we did take off and landed in Orlando. The company had a rental car at the airport for us; all we had to do was find the house. The house was donated to the organization from a family that lost a loved one to cancer. The house was nice and spacious and had a heated pool. In our package, they gave us $1000 in cash and tickets to all the attractions. We also had time to travel across the state to visit her mother and father, who were down in Florida for the winter months. Lori was doing ok. Some days she looked a little weak, but once we got to the amusement parks she perked up. She was always on the go. I was a little tired and I gained a little more weight. That was because of my nerves, I was eating at night and going to bed. *I had no choice at the time, the wife came first and whatever time I had left was for myself.* We were having a great time, we rekindled a romantic dinner we had on our honeymoon in one of the parks. There was some romance that week, but not much because we were so tired from all the walking. By the time we got home we were exhausted. Lori was having a great time and it kept her mind clear of going to the doctors when we got back. Walking together hand-in-hand or arm-in-arm was all I needed that week, just to see her smile and enjoying life. That to me was the greatest gift I ever got. I loved her so much and just wanted her to have fun, which she did.

We came home a couple of days later. It was a great respite for her. The next week, we went back to the doctors. She got her blood work done; the doctor came into the room and told her she was in remission. Everything look great. He said to Lori, "I'll see you back here in two months." So that meant sometime in the beginning of May. Lori was overjoyed. I was very happy for her, almost crying, but in the back of my mind I was still on guard. She was still sick and she had lost a lot of weight. I only think she was around 95 pounds; she was normally about 120 pounds all her life.

My son gave Lori another vacation from me. He sent her back down to Florida for a week with her parents at their home. Our daughter also had spring break down in Florida that week too, so she wanted to meet up with her mother since it had been months since she last saw her. In the meantime, I remodeled Lori's kitchen as a surprise for her. Where Alexis was staying with her friends was about two hours away from Lori; so they planned a day to meet up. They were going to the zoo. That day I received a phone call from my daughter, she was crying. As I was trying to understand what the hell she was saying on the phone, she finally calmed down and said, "Mommy had a seizure and she fainted at the

Stairways

zoo. The emergency responders are coming now and we are going to the hospital." I told Alexis to put her grandmother on the phone. With the ambulance on its way to Lori, I told my mother-in-law to tell them about Lori's history. She said, "Wait Steven, the paramedics want to talk to you." So I told them what was going on and what to check for. They did, and sure enough at the hospital they found out she was dehydrated and her iron was low. A couple of hours later, Lori called me to thank me. I said, "For what, honey?" "Just for helping me out. Even though you are hundreds of miles away, you're still taking care of me." I then asked her, "Are you feeling ok?" "Yes!" She said. She was out eating with her parents, Alexis, and her friends. She said, she smelt sulfur and that was the last thing she remembered. Well, we will honestly never know if that really caused it, but she was okay now, though sadly my daughter had to leave that day.

Lori was coming home in two days; I finished the kitchen in time. New lights new island. Now, to go pick her up. I went to the florist and bought two dozen red roses and one white rose. I got to the Airport; she had a 9:00 PM flight. I got there early I waited at the gate with the roses. The plane pulled in, the passengers were coming off. Most of the ladies coming off the plane were telling me that she's one lucky woman. My answer to all of them: you don't know how lucky I am to have her as a wife. She finally got off the plane; she dropped her bags and ran to me. We embraced with a hug and kiss. "For me?", she said. "No, they're for the flight attendants," I said. She laughed. Lori looked fabulous: white skintight pants, sandals, blue sleeveless blouse, and a white jacket. She was gorgeous. I said jokingly to Lori, "Do you wanna go to a hotel?" She said sure, but home would be better. So we started home. I asked her how she was feeling. She stated she was better. I told her I had one more surprise for her at home. She asked me what, of course. I said she'll have to wait. We arrived home, she went inside and saw her new kitchen. She was elated. I didn't think she would get that excited, but she did and she thanked me. Lori had a lot of energy that night; I guess she was glad to be home. I ran a bath for her; I added lavender bath salts to the water. She sat in the tub and I took a washcloth and washed her back, then her front, and down her legs to her feet. Her eyes were closed, but she took a peek every once in a while. "I'm done.", I told her. "So soon?", she said in a playful voice. "I'll be waiting for you in bed," I told her. She said okay. She came into bed and I told her to lie on her stomach and I'd rub her back, then she could turn over and I'd take care of that too. It was nice. Finally, I could tease and taunt her. She was relaxing and cherishing the moment, and do you blame her?

Some weeks went by. Lori occasionally had some belly aches. I called the doctor and he gave her a prescription for some pain pills. She was taking them when she needed to. She also had to take vitamins and an iron a pill, but that was it, no other medicines. Weekends were for Lori and I. We usually went to the casino, had dinner and then saw a show. Sometimes we stayed over and those were nice moments. Other times we would just go straight home, nothing beats your own bed.

Come springtime, Lori was always asking me to take her to flower farms. Lori was a true green thumb. A couple years back, I took half my backyard and designed her an English Garden. It had walkways and a bridge over a stream that poured into a little pond. I also made her a meditation spot in the corner of her garden which had a table, two chairs, and a fountain. She loved sitting there in the morning with a cup of tea listening to the water and watching hummingbirds take nectar from her flowers. It was peaceful and tranquil for her. Then a couple of months later, I was bored, so I built her an outside room with a full kitchen, an island, outdoor TV, and fireplace. It was all for her. I just enjoyed doing things for her. She really didn't nag, maybe about money from time to time though. I was probably doing all the complaining anyway. We went to the doctors, May had crept up quick, and she got her blood work done. The doctor came in and said she had to start chemo again. She wasn't happy. Her hair was just starting to grow back, and now she'll lose it again. My poor wife. I asked so many times to give me what she had, so she wouldn't have to endure this. Lori sat in the chair to start chemo. She sent me out to get her food and coffee, that was her usual thing when we went there. I usually got her more than she wanted. *That's how I was.* I put a blanket on her when I got back; I tried to lay down on the same recliner with her. I'd snuggle with her while watching TV. On occasion, the nurse would come by and, if we'd fallen asleep together, she would draw the curtains for our privacy. There were times I couldn't do that because the chair was only for one person and they didn't want me to break it. I would make the best out of a bad situation for her. Then we would leave, arm-in-arm or hand-in-hand and say goodbye until next time. When we were leaving the nurses always had Lori's next appointment card ready for her. Lori never wanted to wait. Usually, a week or two after chemo, I would have to drive her back to the hospital. It didn't matter what time it was, she needed fluids. She would dehydrate and sometimes they would give her three or four bags of IV solution because she was so tiny. Chemo drains all the fluids from your body, it's a poison.

Springtime had come and gone. Lori already had her flowers planted, and summertime was here now. After I'd come home from work, Lori and I would jump on our boat at night and ride out into the bay to watch the sun go down. We would just drift with the tide, sometimes two or three miles. We'd be sitting together or she'd sit on my lap, her head on my shoulders, her arms around my neck. I'd be rubbing her back or her feet and she'd drift off into a dream. Or, we would be kissing with the wind blowing at our backs, a blanket around us. *Sheer love.* We were on the boat one day when she whispered in my ear, "Why does it have to end?" I said to her, "There is no end, and there will never be an end with us, we keep going. You know what I mean?" "Yes", she said. Summer was going by quickly. There were a lot of rainy weekends where you almost felt like you were in England with all the storms. July 20th came, our 29th wedding anniversary. Unfortunately, I had to take Lori to the hospital again. She was dehydrated and she felt so bad. We were supposed to go to New York City for the weekend. "It's ok", I told her. "I'll take you in October." She said she was sorry again. "One more *'I'm sorry'* from you and you'll be sorry!", I said shaking my finger at her. She laughed and smiled. Shortly after the hospital visit, we went home. The following day I took her out for dinner.

Weeks turned into months for Lori and me. She looked tired, weak, and frail; something was going on. She started taking extra doses of her pain medication. I called the doctor told him what was going on. He had a talk with Lori; we came to terms about regulating the dosage and the amount she took. Lori said, "I love you, honey," and I replied, "I love you too." "I'm just trying to help you. Don't you understand that?", I said. It wasn't that she was mad at me, it was just that I found out she was abusing the pain pills.

Time was passing. One of Lori's favorite times of the year besides fall was Halloween. She would decorate the house, have her spell book full of full size candy bars out for the kids, but not this year. I had to drive her to the hospital again. She was in great pain, her abdomen had swollen up again. They gave her pain meds through a port in her chest. That past September I had Lori get the port put in because the injections were too traumatic for her every time she went for chemo. The nurses had to find a vein in her arm, but Lori's veins would roll because she was so skinny. They admitted Lori overnight. I slept in the waiting room a couple of doors away. That morning, they drained the fluid from her abdomen. A couple of hours later we went home. She was tired, so was I, but it wasn't about me it was all about Lori. For three years, I'd been caring for her and if it was going to take another three years, I would do just the same. Lori slept on her reclining couch, it was almost like a chase lounge and she loved it. I would sleep on the couch next to her every night and she would watch TV all night. This had started a couple months back. Our master bedroom was now just a place to get dressed or to take a bath or shower; I don't know what will become of our room not just yet, maybe a storage room.

The weekend was upon us and Lori was packed and ready to go to New York City a day early. We were celebrating a belated 29th wedding anniversary. Lori couldn't wait to go. She called me at work that Friday to make sure I was leaving early. I told her I'd see her in the afternoon. I arrived home, she was already done up: make up, hair, dressed, packed. She told me to hurry up and take a shower. She had already packed my belongings, she had never done that before. Before I knew it, we were off. She was like a little kid in a candy store, smiling, kissing, hugging, and she kept grabbing my ass. She told me everything was booked. "Oh, really? Let's hear it.", I said. She was so excited saying these words; "We're staying at the Marriott Time Square, we're going to see Motown: The Musical, were eating at Gordon Ramsey's London, and we're going shopping. "Oh, really?" I said. "What, no sex?" "Oh, I got that planned, too." she said. *What a woman, I said to myself.* Lori was so organized, full of emotion, smiling and happy, but yet she was still fighting a demon inside of her and she didn't show it. I made sure she had all her pills. I was on guard, but I didn't want her to sense anything. I just wanted her to have fun and relax. We got through Friday traffic. Valet took the car and we went to check in. The hotel gave us two days of free breakfast and drink cards for the bar. The bellhop took our luggage. Lori must've packed a week's worth of clothes in those suitcases, but who cares, a woman needs her clothes. Lori and I got on the elevator to the 35th floor and were shown to our room. I tipped the bellhop and picked her up. She moved her legs up and down, like a kid saying 'let me down'. I carried her through the door, the bellhop said have a great weekend, and the door closed behind us.

I laid her on the bed, she gave me a long kiss and whispered "I love you." I dimmed the lights and opened the curtains. What a view of Times Square and Central Park, it was going to be a great weekend. She was all ready to go out and shop. I said, "Can you give me a chance?" She told me, "Hurry up." Two minutes later, we were gone. Lori went into practically every store, from her favorite lingerie shop to her favorite department store. She was looking for riding boots and she finally found them in a small boutique down in the village. The price of the boots, you ask? Let's just say it was a small fortune. I didn't mind spending the money. You understand, money doesn't buy happiness, health, or love. Lori was now dragging me to a toy store, she wanted to go on the Ferris wheel and then eat at a restaurant for lunch. I never knew I could pay $25.00 for a hamburger. Found out it was Kobe beef after paying the $85.00 bill for lunch. Next, it was off to Central Park for a carriage ride. That ride was about an hour long. Something about carriages brought me back to a dream I had early in my youth with Lori. I don't know what it was about carriages, maybe it was something we shared in another life? I don't know. The carriage ride we were experiencing was nothing but romantic. It was a cool day outside, so we needed a blanket drawn over us. After the ride, it was back to more shopping and finally we got back to the hotel. *I needed to get another suitcase just for what she bought.* That night we took it easy and went to the bar and had a drink or two and retired to bed. The following day, the hotel had a breakfast fit for a king and queen. You name it, they had it, from poached eggs to salmon. I'm pretty sure this was not included in the hotel bill, but I didn't care. I wanted to make sure that, God forbid, if this was our last anniversary together that she would remember it. So off we went sightseeing like we would do on Christmas Eve. Uptown, downtown, I was exhausted. Finally, we got back to the hotel. Lori took a bath and I took a shower. Lori got dressed, she went all out for dinner. This time she had on a blue dress, so tight and just above the knees, high heels, and a new wig. It was one of those wigs that reminded me of the 80s and she was stunning as usual. I put on my suit, no tie. Lori hated ties. I grabbed her coat. She said, "Wait a minute." She walked over to me with a model like walk, she put her arms around my neck, I grabbed her waist and we embraced. "Happy anniversary," I whispered. "I love you," she said softly. Jokingly, I said, "Ditto!" She laughed, because I was referring to a movie we used to watch, and the lead actor used to say that to his girlfriend after she said I love you. We had a long kiss and proceeded to go to the bar before dinner. Lori had a cosmo and I had a martini and a beer. I put her coat on after our drinks. It was a cold and windy night. We went outside, I hailed a cab and off we went to the restaurant.

What a place it was, I can just imagine the bill. *But then again, I didn't care.* The maître d' sat us at a table for two, the lights were dimmed. A single candle lit our table, the reflection of the flame danced in her eyes. She looked a little tired, but she said she wasn't. We got our drinks and I made a little toast to Lori, "Happy Anniversary; I love you as you are and will always love you. I will use my heart to provide you the love you need and the care that you may require till death do us part." The tears trickled down her cheeks. "I love you so much," she whispered. We knocked our glasses together and she ordered dinner for both of us, Oysters Rockefeller as an appetizer and chateaubriand for two. I never saw Lori eat so much, even without that stomach of hers. We were so full that we didn't even order desert, but the restaurant knew it was our anniversary and they brought us over a cake with a candle. We blew the candle out at the same time while holding hands. I paid the bill, hailed a cab, and I asked Lori if she wanted to go anywhere else. She said, "Yes, to bed with you!" So I told the driver to hurry up. Lori started to laugh. We arrived at the hotel, entered the elevator, and pushed the button. The doors closed and we started making out. The doors opened and I carried her to the room, we went inside. I got comfortable; she went into the bathroom with a package. I opened the curtains, dimmed the lights. Lori came out of the bathroom in the white silk gown she wore on our wedding night. She had no wig on. She said, "Why do I need it on?" "That's true." I said. She lied down next to me on the bed. While I was rubbing her back, I was thinking that whether she had hair or no hair, whether she was skinny or fat, she's still my wife and I loved her so. She may not think she's attractive or beautiful looking anymore, but she's still my wife. Lori looked at me and said, "What's the matter, honey?" "Nothing, Lori.", I said to her. She put her arms around me and held me tight and whispered "It's ok." We just held each other for a while and talked about what's next for us. This meant whether we wanted to move or not when our daughter, Alexis, graduated college in May. We didn't' know what the future had in store for us. All of a sudden it started to storm outside. The rain and the lightning only added to our evening romance. In the morning we had breakfast again, shopped a little, went to see a show and then headed home.

Thanksgiving was already around the corner. Alexis was home from college for the week. She helped Lori cook Thanksgiving dinner that year; it's not like she didn't help before, but this year it was more than ever. Lori was physically weak, but mentally strong. I kept in constant touch with the doctor's office at least once a week. They said I was one of the few caregivers that would call to give them updates. They said they would worry when people didn't call. Lori was very skinny. She weighed about eighty pounds or so at 5'6. She was very drawn; she hadn't been eating much, at least not in front of me. I mentioned it to her constantly, and it made her mad. I understand now it must have been so annoying, being an adult and having someone asking you questions and telling you what to do. *It was my job to take care of her.* "Well, I'm the boss," she said, "so stop!" That's basically what Lori told me every time I badgered her. I just walked away. I went outside to the basement, grabbed a baseball and started throwing it as hard as I could against the concrete wall. Eventually, the cover of the ball ripped open just like my heart was being ripped open. But hearts can't be sewn back together. The woman I fell in love with at fourteen years old is slowly dying and neither I nor anybody else can stop it. I just knew it. I had that gut-feeling inside. I must be strong for her though, even if I just wanted to break down.

Company finally came. We gave thanks at the table for health, love, and happiness. The food was good as usual; Lori made massive amounts of food per usual. She made so many dishes and, of course, the turkey was tender as usual. Night fell and company left. The kids did the dishes and cleaned up. Lori and I took a walk outside down the street. She asked me if I thought everybody enjoyed the food. I said to her, "Everybody looks forward to coming to our house when you cook. Of course they enjoyed it, there's nothing left." She never asked me that question before. Maybe she thought she had lost her touch, but she hadn't.

Lori had another appointment for chemo. I couldn't take her this time, so her mother did. When I got home, the first thing I noticed was that both Lori and her mother had blank faces on, no expressions. "Okay, what's going on?" I said. Lori said to me, "The doctor said the chemotherapy I am getting now doesn't seem to be working, and he didn't want me to get it this time. He wants to do a new type of chemo the day after Christmas." *What else?* There was nothing else. Bullshit, I said to myself. I took a walk down the street and called the doctor's office. I insisted on talking to the doctor. The doctor got on the phone and told me that the chemo wasn't working and that it was because her blood levels were all over the place. "So, what's next?" I said. He said, "48 hours of chemotherapy, that she will take at home for a day. Then, we will send the nurse to take the needle out once the procedure is complete. You will also be trained to give her IV fluids." Well, that was it, and I said okay. I asked him if he would tell me what her chances were. *What a hard question it was.* "Well Steve, she's taken a lot. I don't know, but she's done well in the past with other treatments, let's see how this one goes." *Let's see how it goes.*

It's was now about two weeks before Christmas. Usually, Lori and I would go and cut a tree down, but not this year. It was just too much. I went to the local store and bought a seven foot tree. In prior years, Lori would yell at me for putting up a fourteen foot tall tree in the house. I had to start decorating. Lori was really weak and really couldn't. I did all the necessary decorating around the house, even the tree. Lori would always hang her Victorian ornaments on the tree. The ornaments were all collectors' items that Lori has been buying ever since we got married. Alexis did a great job baking. Lori and I also used to wrap all the presents in our room with the door shut with a glass of wine. This year, Alexis did it. She even wrapped her own gifts. I did some as well with a cup of coffee by my side. Lori went with Alexis to the store during that week. She wanted to get little stocking stuffers for all of us. She sent Alexis to buy my Christmas gifts too. Most of the time Lori just sat on the couch and watched TV. She said to all of us, "It's about time you guys did things yourself." God, I said to myself, please give her the strength to go on. She had never said things like that before. *She was right though.*

Christmas Eve was here. It was a rainy, gloomy day, but that didn't stop us. Lori got her energy back. She wanted to go to New York City, as we did as a family for many years. This year Lori bought tickets to a show. We always tried to switch things up a little. One year we went to the wax museum, another we saw the Freedom Tower.

The Christmas show started at 11:00 AM, we were late. That was partly my fault, though, because I didn't want to go to New York this year. Honestly, I didn't know how Lori would be. Like always, I did everything I could to please her. So we went. I dropped the kids and Lori off at the front door then parked the car. We had middle front row seats; everybody enjoyed it. Lori kept falling asleep during the show and it made me upset. It made the kids upset. I sat next to Alexis and she kept watching me cry. We didn't want to wake her up; she got up herself, when she was ready, and enjoyed the show.

After the show, Lori was looking at souvenirs and came across a Christmas bear with a bow in its hair. "Do you want that, honey?" I asked her. She always loved stuffed animals and little knickknacks. "Yes, sweetheart!" she said. So I bought her the bear. Next we did a little shopping as the day went on. It was raining on and off. Luckily, we had umbrellas. We saw the tree at Rockefeller center. We went to eat, not at our usual place though. The food was still good. Lori ate some of her lobster, the kids ate well too. I wasn't too hungry, but we were a family enjoying a meal and for that brief moment everything was okay. I was still on guard, I had to be. She was so frail that she had to hold onto me to walk. I kept my emotions as best I could, though in reality all I wanted to do was cry. My willpower carried me. We left early; it was just raining too hard and Lori was tired. The two things we didn't get to do, were go to church and have our carriage ride around Central Park. I told her that, come springtime, we would go for that carriage ride. Lori was fine with that, she just didn't want to get wet.

We went home; the two kids and Lori fell asleep in the car. At that moment, I somehow felt alone driving, like they all weren't even in the car. *Is this what it would be like by myself?* I was scared just thinking about it. I cried inside myself thinking that this could possibly happen, my wife passing away and my adult children left motherless. What a terrible feeling it gave me and it all could happen. *Was I prepared?*

We got home early, we open presents. Lori bought me a vacuum, of all things. I am a clean fanatic. I broke the last vaccum. Lori said to me, "This is the last one I'm ever going to buy you, so don't break it." She also got me a blue tooth speaker and some other little things. I gave Lori money, a card and a gift certificate for spray tanning. The kids got what they wanted and then we all retired to bed. The following day we went to Lori sister's house for Christmas dinner. It was a short stay though because Lori was tired and chemo was happening the next day. One of the relatives came over to me and whispered in my ear, "That's not the Lori I know," and then she walked away. I didn't know how to react. So I went outside and cried, saying my prayers to the night sky. We went home; the kids stayed a while longer. I walked with Lori hand-in-hand to the front door, we went inside. I got her undressed and laid her down on the couch. I gave her a kiss and then she fell asleep. I slept next to her on the other couch. One eye open, one eye shut; that's the way it was. The following morning I had to work, so our son Chris took Lori to chemo. I called him later in the day, he said everything was ok; he was at the store with Lori. He told me that she had a pump connected to her port that was feeding her drugs and that she would have to wear it until Saturday afternoon, then the nurse would come over and remove it. Lori seemed to tolerate it quite well. The next couple of days I had to give her fluids so she wouldn't dehydrate.

New Year's Eve was here and Alexis went back to school. Chris was out with his friends and Lori and I, well, it's the first time in a long time we stayed home. She laid down in bed, and watched TV. I was in the family room watching the ball drop. At the 12:00 hour I went to our room and gave Lori a hug and a kiss. "Happy New Year, sweetheart", I said. She said the same thing and drifted off to sleep. I shut the TV off and lay next to her. The last time we were in bed together was on our 29th anniversary trip to New York City in October. I watch my wife sleep that entire night. All night I watched her breathe, thinking when will that last breath come out. Will I ever be able to say goodbye to her, or to say that I've loved her and adored her our entire life together?

Steven Zarycki

HOW LONG, DOCTOR?

Two days passed, Lori was eating a little and I was on guard. I was giving her fluids and some normal routine medications. It was now Sunday and Lori was having pains in her abdomen. I called the doctors that were on standby. They told me to try and get her to go to the bathroom and to give her a heating pad. The doctors knew that she probably used too many pain pills and that she may have been backed up from doing so. I was doing everything I possibly could that day for Lori. Trying to keep her comfortable and pain free was my first priority. The night was falling, Lori's pain lessened a bit through the night and she finally fell asleep. I fell asleep on the couch. I woke up early Monday morning around 5am; she was up with the TV on. She said, she had pains on and off through the night. "Why didn't you wake me up?" I asked her. She explained that she didn't want to wake me up because I was tired and she could see it in my eyes. "Bull, I'm your husband and caregiver. It doesn't matter if I'm tired or not, you have to wake me up. Damn, Lori, don't do this again." "Listen," she said to me, "you go to work and if I have more pain you can take me to the hospital tonight." I called Lori probably about four or five times that day; she detested me when I would do that. She said the pain was a little less, but when I finally got home she looked pale. So I got her dressed, packed the bag, and left for the hospital.

I arrived at the emergency room in about an hour. I already called the doctor and they knew we were coming: Lori walked in by herself. I parked the car, and then ran into the emergency room. They already took her into one of the rooms and started taking her vitals. They drew blood from her port on her chest, gave her an IV bag and two milligrams of Dilaudid. That relaxed her a lot. Of all things, she said she was hungry. We had to wait though because of the blood tests. The doctor on staff came in and said her white blood cells were low and she needed iron, so they went ahead and gave her a blood transfusion.

I was basically running on coffee that day. They were going to admit her. We had to wait for a room: it was 1:30 AM. Lori was resting, my body was tired and my emotions drained. I felt helpless, what could I do. *Nothing, I said to myself. She's in the best care. Stop worrying, Steve.* Lori kept telling me to go home and sleep. She knew I had to work the next day and said I could come back after work. I didn't want to go. I didn't want to leave her side. She got mad. "You go, now! I'll call you when they put me into my room," she stated. "Okay, you win", I said to her. We then exchanged an 'I love you, honey' and an 'I love you too, sweetheart', gave each other a hug and kiss, and I left. By this time it was now 3:00 AM. The drive home was killing me with songs that kept playing on the car radio from the 1980s. All they kept doing was making me think of all the times Lori and I had together. Yeah, I could've shut off the radio but I didn't. I wanted to relive those memories, to feel the love and happiness we had all through those years. I just wanted to listen and reminisce.

Finally I got home; she called me at 5:00 AM. "You ok?" I asked her. "Yes," she said with a drug induced voice. "I'm in my room, I'm going to sleep, and I love you. See you after work." By this time I'd been up for nearly twenty-four hours, no sleep, and couldn't wait to leave work. I called Lori's mother and told her what was going on. I cried while talking to her, she knew I was at the end of my rope, and that I was drained and just about to lose it. I have to be strong and keep the faith, always trying to keep positive. I knew in the back of my mind that we'd just started to lose the battle. It hurt so much; *my heart was slowly bleeding for Lori.*

I arrived back at the hospital, she had a private room. She had a little slur in her speech from the pain medications. She got out a, "Hi, honey. I love you." I cheered up. I came over to her by her bed, gave her a hug and a kiss, and she put her arms around my back and started rubbing it. She kept telling me to relax and that she was okay. But my heart kept telling me that she wasn't, and it started to split down the middle. All I could do was pray in silence to myself.

I was able to stay that night because she had the private room. In the morning, the doctors came in to check on her. They told us that she's was on a regimen to keep her blood stable. I called work told them I wouldn't be in the rest of the week and they understood. It was now Wednesday morning, January 7th, 2015. I was up all night before watching her and making sure things were going right. Who was doing what and who was giving her what: you always have to be on watch. "Morning, honey," I said to her. "Morning, sweetheart," Lori said to me. Would you like some coffee this morning? She told me sure. I went downstairs to the cafeteria and got her some coffee. Lori developed an open wound by her coccyx bone from sliding up and down on the bed. She couldn't get comfortable unless there were pillows under her or an air mattress, which the nurses finally brought in. Lori and I were having small talk. Something wasn't right, she was a little incoherent and that wasn't her normal. The doctors told me it was from the pain pills or it might be chemo brain. The doctors told me that the chemotherapy might've been too strong for her.

    I said to Lori, "Honey, do you know what today is?" "No, not really.", she responded. I told her it was our day, January 7, the day when she and I meet forty years ago. It was the day we met and fell in love on the basement stairs of your house. After that first kiss together, she hugged me so tight and whispered in my ear that I was the one. Lori's eyes turn glassy, she knew the date, and she wanted to see if I remembered. I gave Lori a kiss on her forehead, on both cheeks and then, on her lips. After that moment, Lori's doctor then came in. In a quick motion I wiped the tears away from her eyes. He sat down to talk to us. He told us that they were trying to stabilize her blood and it wasn't looking good. I looked at Lori. She did not understand or maybe she did, or maybe she was just in shock. The doctor said it could be possible that things might turn around but he had his doubts. I left Lori alone for a while; I went to the waiting room with the doctor. Then I broke down. "How long, doc?" I said with a shaking voice. He said, "Steve, it could be a couple of days or weeks. I don't know, I'm so sorry. It's been a long battle for Lori and you." He got up and gave me a hug. He then explained to me that he would be sending me a palliative team of doctors to see Lori and I and to arrange hospice at home. He left the room; that's when the walls closed in on my entire life and the life I had made with the love of my life. I was numb with the news, my emotions uncontrollable. I went to the bathroom, washed my face, then looked in the mirror and shook my head in dismay. I took a deep breath and went back into the room to see my wife. She was incoherent, maybe from the drugs or maybe the cancer had spread to her brain. There was really no more need for any more tests. This was it. No more calling to make appointments or calling them to tell them how she's doing. I'm going to bring my wife home so she can die in comfort, with me and her beloved family by her side.

The first call I made was to her mother and father. I've been with Lori's family since I was 14 years old and now I'm 53, they were like my second parents. They let Lori and I experience God's gift, to learn, to understand, and most of all, love at such an early age. I remember my mother-in-law calling my mother about a month after Lori and I started dating. She said, "Jean, I just want to tell you there is something between your son and my daughter, and not to interfere. Let nature take its course." I remember that because my wife told me she was eavesdropping on the conversation at the time. And you know what, we did! We learned. Like a stairway, Lori and I called it. Sometimes you climb to the top, then you have to come back down, or you have to stop halfway to think about things. Lori and I knew that life was full of ups and downs. Her mother answered the phone, "Hi, sweetie.", she said to me with a bounce in her voice." "Ma." I said. I started to break down. "Lori," I said crying, "they only gave her a couple of days to a couple of weeks to live, I need you to come home from Florida to me. I don't think I can do this anymore by myself. I need help, please come home to your daughter."

"Steve," she said, "relax, and stay strong, we'll get a flight back as soon as possible. Remember, we love you." The next call was to Cathy, Lori's best friend. It was hard to talk to her about this because I knew she would be going through the same dilemma with her husband later on in life. Her husband was fighting his own battle with cancer too. "Steve, whatever you need, I'm here for you and Lori," she said. I called my parents as well as my cousins. Whoever I could think of that lived close, I called. I called my son, he asked me if I called Alexis. " No!" I said. I was trying to find the words to tell her to ease the pain. She just left to go back to school just before New Year's. I didn't want to regret as a father not getting her back home to her mother, or her as a daughter to regret not being home with her mother in what could be her last few days. So I called her and explained the chain of events that happened after she went back to school. "Okay, Dad", she said. She's just like her mother, strong willed. Thank God for my children being so much like their mother; I love them both.

The next morning the special care team came into the room to talk about hospice. The team set everything up for us at home including a nurse, medicines, a care worker, a social worker, and a chaplain. But you know, the real hospice was going to be Lori's family with me as her main caregiver. I wanted to make sure my soul mate got nothing but the best care for whatever amount of time she had left on this earth. We were the best people to deliver that to her.

 Relatives started coming to the hospital the following day to visit. It felt to me almost like they were paying their last respects, but I know it wasn't true. They were here for me as well as Lori, for support, for my family, and I love them all for that. Lori's girlfriend, Cathy, came with her husband. She said she arranged to get Lori home tomorrow with an ambulance that my hometown supplied. The day went slow which was ok. It was more time for me to spend with my wife. The next morning was rough, Lori knew she was going home and I think she also knew she was never coming back to the hospital again. The nurses and doctors knew of Lori and I and the battle we fought together for three plus years. They knew of the love I had for Lori and the love she had for me, they were like a family to us. Cathy came with the ambulance. They were waiting outside Lori's room. I got Lori dressed with the nurses and then Lori did something that I'll surely never forget. She said in a slurred voice, "I want to walk." Everyone around us, including myself, was shocked. What my wife wanted, she got. So Cathy and her assistant picked Lori up and started to walk her out of the room. I followed behind, holding back tears as she walked by the nurses' station. A silence came over everyone, even the doctor that told her she only had a few days to live. All the nurses stood up, some with tears in their eyes. The doctor than came around the station window and stood in front of Lori and gave her a hug. Lori gave him a hug back. Then the doctor bent over and whispered something in her ear. I don't know what it was and I wasn't going to ask. All I know was that Lori had a little smile on her face. I gathered all of our belongings. Lori was transported home with her best friend, Cathy, by her side. I told them I would meet them at home. Leaving the hospital by myself was hard enough; the entire staff gathering to say goodbye to me was even harder. They knew Lori and I would never be back again. For three solid years, they took care of my wife. She was cared for with dignity and respect. She received nothing but the best from Penn Medicine. They treated her as if she was a human being, not a patient.

Stairways

THERE IS NO ENDING

I'm home now, just waiting for the ambulance to arrive with Lori. I have some time to myself now. I stood quietly in the center of our home, making a complete circle while standing in one spot. *This place was us,* I thought to myself. No, this home was *Lori,* from the paint on the walls, to the pictures scattered everywhere, to the flowers in the vases on the table; *this was all Lori.* This was her dream that she wrote to me in a love letter from high school. That was a long time ago when she wrote it, and it all came true. I kept thinking and saying to myself that if and when Lori passes away at home…*what am I supposed to do?* I really was at a loss for words. I was starting to feel lost in this entire life of mine without *her.*

I could see the lights of the ambulance outside the house. *She's here!* I ran to the door and saw Lori was on a stretcher. I told them I wanted to carry her in. "Please hold the door for me", I said to the EMTs. And that's exactly what they did. Lori put her arms around my neck and I picked up her legs and her back and carried her in through the doorway, just like I did when we came home from our honeymoon. She gave me a kiss on the cheek and smiled. I had made her bed with pillows and blankets before she came home. I laid her down on the bed and made her comfortable. Our little Pomeranian, Taffy, jumped upon the bed and laid by Lori's side. Lori and I were home alone until my son Chris came home from work. Chris came into the room where Lori was, and I walked out of the room so they could spend time together as mother and first-born son. I slowly shut the door behind me.

The next couple of days were hectic. Lori's mother and father arrived and so did Alexis. Lori was happy. I, on the other hand, was dealing with hospice, the medical supply deliveries coming to the house, who was coming to visit Lori from our family and on what days, and what I had to do just in case *that day* came. The days went by very fast. I kept an hourly and daily journal on what Lori ate and what pain she had; a general description on how she was feeling. She was on one pain pill every four hours, and that was just for that open wound on her butt, which was a bed sore. It was kind of funny in a way; Lori knew every 4 hours when she was due for another pill, even though she was only semi-coherent of her surroundings. Jo Ann, Lori's mother, continued to stay with us. Her father, Tony, stayed at Lori's sister's house in the next town over from us. Our house was full of love and people that Lori loved and cared for; truly that was the best medicine for her. I was working every day, trying to keep my mind active, but I was still calling home every hour to check up on Lori's status. During the next couple of days, Lori had more visitors than you could count. Uncles, aunts, cousins and friends, you name it. I know in my heart that all who showed up to the house were not paying their last respects to Lori, but were showing my family that they all cared for us and truthfully loved our family. They gave us their strength and support, which we needed immensely.

Even though Lori was diagnosed as terminal, she was a busy lady. She wanted to get out of the house as much as she could, even to go grocery shopping. Alexis would take her out on these mini-adventures. Lori walked as best as she could inside the stores, but always with assistance. Finally, a wheelchair arrived from hospice and Lori thought she was free to go anywhere she wanted to. That was good! However, it was winter and the cold wasn't good for her. One day I came home from work, a long day as a matter of fact, and my children explained to me that Lori wanted to go to Atlantic City. I said to myself, *are you kidding*? My children convinced me that it was best for Lori to enjoy these little things that made her happy. Though I was a bit reluctant at first, my children were right and I said, "Let's go" in a monotone voice. As exhausted and overworked as I was, I took Lori and the kids down to Atlantic City. I lifted her out of the car, put her in the wheelchair, and off to the casino we went. I sat her down by her favorite machine and she played…and played…and played. She lost a little here and there, but then she came back and won over $100. *I couldn't believe it.* After about 2 hours, we decided to leave. Lori was a little mad because we were leaving early. It was 10:30 PM and I was just so tired that I couldn't even concentrate. I had to go to work the next day, and Lori didn't really understand that. But, as I look back on it, I'm glad we went and spent that time together, despite all the obstacles.

I was having such a hard time with sleep and my emotions. My world, or should I say *our world*, was coming to an end. I didn't know when it was going to happen. I didn't want it to happen, but it was on my mind *every day*. When I woke up each morning next to her, I had to check her. I would give her a kiss on the lips and say I love you and go to work. It was hard for me to close that door behind me every morning, knowing today might be the last day that I will be able to see her alive or to say *I love you* to Lori. I came home that day from work. "Dad, Mom wants to go to her favorite restaurant in Atlantic City," said my daughter. "Are you kidding me?" I asked, with an exhaustive tone. My daughter Alexis was as persistent as Lori was. I paused, thought about it, took a deep breath and said, "Ok...let's go." I loaded up the car with Lori's wheelchair and her medical supplies and away we went back down to Atlantic City for a second day in a row. Lori loved fondue, so we headed to the fondue restaurant she enjoyed. She ordered steak and lobster, of all things, and a cosmopolitan as a drink. Looking at her that night, she smiled at me and blew me a kiss. I told her, "Live it up, honey! You deserve it!" After dinner Lori wanted to gamble, again. She also wanted saltwater taffy. As fatigued as I was, I couldn't say no to her demands. Even though I was weary, worried, depressed, and emotional, she came first. Who knew if she would have the chance to come back again? So, my daughter and Lori's mother took her to get some saltwater taffy and then play a few machines. We went to the casino that night where Lori and I loved to gamble, as did my children and Lori's mother. Lori, as weak as she was, enjoyed herself to the fullest extent and it turned out to be a positive and blissful night.

 Lori and I were planning a trip to Antigua for our 30th wedding anniversary in July of 2015 to renew our vows. While she was on hospice care, Lori ordered two new dresses and a new suitcase for the trip. All I could do is shrug my shoulders in despair and understand that Lori would probably never get to wear them. When the items arrived at the house, I thought about how I would have to most likely return them; but I knew I wouldn't. Lori also spent some time online shopping with my daughter, whom I knew would get the dresses if Lori didn't. They lay in bed together buying pajamas, which were one of Lori's favorite things. They sat together buying things, things I knew she may never wear. But as my children reiterated to me, it didn't matter as long as Lori was happy.

 The next couple of days Lori watched television from her wheelchair and was eating a little bit more. Most of her pain was caused by the exposed wound on her backside. I was thankful that she had no stomach pain. I would have to address her exposed wound once a day, other times Lori's mother, or my children would do it for me. The weekend was here and the house seemed normal for once. My family all together, the house calm and full of love. Lori continued to watch television, sleep, and eat in her favorite chase lounge chair. By now, it was a daily routine to clean, dress, and feed my wife.

As I had mentioned before, my wife Lori was the most independent woman I knew. She loathed people doing these things for her. It was so upsetting to see this, not only for me, but it was heartbreaking for the entire family. I soon realized that when a person is dying they somehow transform back to when they were a baby, when the parents would have to take care of them. Every waking day, one member of the family or Lori's closest friend, Kathy, would take turns caring for her. I was the primary caregiver. To have to watch the person who was my soul mate dying slowly in front of me was painful. However, I swore a vow when we were married to care for her, in sickness and in health.

In all honestly, I never thought in a million years that this would be the way our life together would end. As a husband, I adored and loved my wife so much. I provided for her. I protected her. From such an early age, I grew up with Lori. It was as if we were meant to be together, like a fairy tale that had no ending. But all good things do come to an end. And still to this day I can't understand why? For years I heard of people getting sick and dying, never thinking it would happen to either one of us. Maybe we thought we were indestructible as partners. But death, as I've come to learn, is part of life. I also, however, know that it came too soon in ours. We wanted so much more out of life. I wanted to grow old with her, see our children get married, and have grandchildren to play with. Knowing it probably wasn't going to be like that, well it broke me.

I'll say one thing though, Lori and I showed love to each other every day of life together. Whether it was on one of our adventures or at home, love was always there. And as a caregiver, well, it's a job within itself. You have to have the strength and courage to keep going for your partner. You find it deep inside yourself. Even if you say you can't do this anymore, you have to find the will to do so. You may be breaking down inside, looking at the one your caring for and saying you can't do it, but you can. That's your loved one. That's the one who took care of you when you were sick, and now they need your help.

I think if there's one thing I want people to know is that you should never be afraid to ask for help. I can tell you right now that I was tired from everything that was going on, but that was my soul mate and she needed me. I had to be strong. Not only for her, but for our children as well. Though, I knew I also had to take care of myself as well, take a break, and let somebody else help me. It was hard for me to leave Lori for just a minute, as it is for anyone who is a caregiver, but you have to take care of yourself too.

Tony, Lori's father, came over occasionally. It was especially hard for him to see his daughter slowly wither away. One could see in his glassy eyes, the agony he was feeling. I think the fact he was very sick a few years back added to his emotions. Death was something he once came close to facing himself and this was his first daughter in the same position. I think every parent would say they would want to die before their children, yet that wasn't an option here. This was his daughter dying there in the living room. I can only imagine his pain, as well as my entire family's pain.

As I was stating before, it was Friday, and the weekend was here. Lori asked me to give her a bath, but then she changed her mind and wanted a shower. I said, "Sure, honey. I'm going to need some help though." I called on my kids and my sister-in-law to help. I carried Lori to the bathroom. Turning the water on slowly in order set it to a warm temperature, my sister-in-law and daughter undressed Lori and held her while I got into the shower. Lori couldn't stand on her own, so I had to be there for her to lean on. I disrobed also, wearing only underwear, and jumped into the shower with my wife. As I held her, my daughter handed me a bar of soap and helped with washing her mother. My son and sister-in-law waited in the bathroom with us. They held up a blanket in front of the shower to give Lori some sort of privacy. My son Chris, who was twenty-seven at the time, was a little embarrassed; he was the one holding the towels. It was a bit comical to them, and I thought a little bit of the same, but it was a very surreal moment for us. Yet, it also showed us how strong our bond as a family was. As Lori slowly tried washing herself, I grabbed the bar of soap from her hands and started washing her from her face to her toes. She let out a little giggle when I did her toes. I guess it tickled her, but hearing her laugh was all I needed. She then took the bar of soap from me and started to wash me, she was smiling the best she could. She dropped the bar of soap. I bent down to pick it up. She told me to leave it alone. Lori then struggled to put her arms around my neck; I drew her close to me and she gave me little kisses on the ear, then on my cheek and then on my lips. I heard a little giggle behind the blanket. I paid no attention to it. Lori whispered in my ear, "Thank you, my love, for all you've done." That's all it took for me to lose my emotions. I just knew, down deep in my heart, that this would be our last romantic time together. The love I felt for Lori was so overwhelming, that I didn't want it to end. I towel dried Lori, then got her dressed and laid her to rest on her lounge chair.

Saturday morning came and my daughter was heading back to school. If there was one thing Lori was persistent about, it was having Alexis finish college. No matter what. It had been two weeks already and she had to get back to school. She had good quality time with her mother. They laughed and cried and Lori told Alexis she wanted her to finish school, whatever happens. She promised her mother she would. I told Alexis, "I'll call you if anything happens honey." "Okay, Daddy," she said. Then I gave her a kiss goodbye and started to cry.

Lori kept asking to go out that day. She wanted to go to Smithville. A place with little shops that she loved. "Ok, let me get you dressed," I said. I put the wheelchair in the car. After Lori kissed Alexis and Chris goodbye, I then carried her to the car, put her in the front seat, buckled her up and off we went.

She fell asleep in the car. Occasionally, I called her name and she woke up. I said to her, "You have anything to say?" She replied with a "You talk to me, honey." So I did just that, and just rambled on and held her hand and played with her fingers. She gave me an air-kiss and I give it back to her. We arrived. I put her in her chair and pushed her around. She went to the candy shop, bought candy and then went to various stores and bought little trinkets here and there. She asked me to take her to lunch at the inn. She told me what she wanted, I ordered it, and we ate. I had to feed her. It was sad, so sad. Only eight months ago we were here for a romantic dinner and she was feeding herself, now look what transpired. During

Easter, she and I and the family had had brunch here for the past couple of years. This year, we would have to see. I took Lori home, carried her inside, took her coat off, laid her on the couch and she fell asleep.

The week went by and Lori was still the same. The nurse came by to check her vitals and to check the log book I was keeping. Lori ate a little less every day and I couldn't do anything about it. It was Tuesday, February 3. I gave my honey a kiss goodbye, and I went to work. My mom and Lori's mom were at the house tending to Lori. I called in the late afternoon to check on her. Lori's mom said, "Lori didn't want to eat and is just sleeping. She seemed restless, always moving around." I said, "I'll be home soon."

Once I arrived home, I said hello to everyone, gave my wife a kiss, and went to the pantry to get a jar of baby food. Baby food was about the only thing Lori could hold down. I spoon fed her and she ate a little. She was at least drinking some juice throughout the day. I sat down beside her. She asked me, "What are you writing about?" I said to her, "That book about us. You remember, I started it in 1986?" She said to me, "I want to read it when you're done." I whispered, "Ok, honey. You will, when I'm done."

Night was falling. I changed Lori for bed and laid down on the couch next to her with the TV on in the living room. I gave her a kiss and told her I loved her. She said the same thing to me. I expressed to her I had to get up at 5:00 AM to go to work early and she whispered to me, "Ok." That morning I woke up, started the coffee, and checked on my wife like I always did. She looked very pale and weak. Something wasn't right. I could see her moving a little and she felt a little cold, even though I had an electrically heated blanket on her. I had this feeling that it was time; she's leaving this world. I woke up Chris and Jo Ann and I told them that Lori was starting to pass away, and to please make the phone calls to our loved ones, my daughter included. Lori wasn't in any distress. I gave her a little shot of morphine and I kneeled by her side at 5:20 AM on February 4th, 2015. I whispered in her ear, "I love you, you can let go now," as she took her last breath.

Stairways

March 7th, 2015

Dear Lord, please hold back my tears so that I might deliver this eulogy at her memorial:

Eulogies are always hard to write. What do you really say? Do you talk about each day of Lori's life and how she spread love and happiness to each of us? Or do you speak of what you forgot to say, and what do you remember to say, or have you painted the full picture, or are there holes in the story of her? I look out at all the faces here this morning and I think to myself that I should say thank you for coming, but then I realize you didn't come here to perform a duty that burdens you to show your respects. Looking into all your eyes and faces, I know it is because you to share in my great loss. But I'm still going to say thank you, to all of you, for coming and celebrating the life's journey of my wife Lori, and the mother of my two children.

I now have two guardian angels: one being my son who sits on my shoulder to keep me out of trouble; the second angel I was married to, so that I would continue to love and honor. I don't know about any one of you, but for me, getting married to Lori and knowing her all my life was the best thing that ever happened to me. We just celebrated 40 years together on January 7th 2015 and would have been married 30 years this July. She was my best friend, my lover, my soul mate. She was the source of all my happiness and all the adventures I had in my lifetime. The best part of each day was waking up to find her by my side, and the best part of each night was going to sleep knowing she was lying next to me, and the best thing about life was knowing no matter how hard things turned out, how scary it was, or how poor we were, that all I had to do was go home, close the door behind me, and see my wife, and nothing else would seem that important any longer.

I guess what they say about your home being your castle is really true, because whenever I got home everything outside my door was no longer of any concern to me. But what they forgot to tell you is your castle is only your home if you have your *best friend* waiting for you and that friend was my wife, Lori. I don't need to tell you about all the good things that were Lori, and I don't need to convince you that she was special, because your being here today tells me she has touched your lives, like she did with me. I will miss her terribly but when I look into my children's eyes and faces, there is a part of her that is still with us.

Well, honey, I'll be ok. I have our children to help me through this. I know in the past you were worried about me being tired and run down, but it's ok. I did my job till death do us part; I just hope I earned my ticket to heaven. Two things out of many, I'll miss is your gourmet cooking. Coming home after work, opening that front door, and being hit with an explosion of smells in the air. You used to try new recipes on me first before you serve the dish to any of our guests, to see if it was good enough to serve. That's one Guinea pig job I will miss.

The drives. The long drives to God-knows-where: Vermont, New York City, Lake George, and of course, Atlantic City, just for a weekend trip, sometimes with just the clothes on our backs. Lori would always say just stop at a drugstore or a department store on the way for supplies. Easy for her to say, I was doing all the driving and looking for the stores. Finally she got smart and kept an overnight bag packed in the trunk of the car. We, together, had a lifetime of memories. Too many to talk about, but I know the two closest memories to both Lori and I besides getting married were the births of our two children. The day before Valentine's Day this year, after Lori's passing, I was in our basement just trying to keep busy and I came across a duffel bag filled with my junk from where I used to live before I got married. I opened it up and found all the love letters I saved that Lori wrote to me when we started dating back in 1977. Talk about memories. I took one of the letters out of the bag and do you believe the first one I read said, "Steven, my sweetheart, Happy Valentine's Day". Talk about a card from heaven.

There's one little poem Lori wrote to me on that same letter that I want to share with you, she called it *Forevermore:* *"You are that special someone in my life. You hold all the keys to my future. Only you unlock my love, so deeply buried inside my soul. You're the one to turn my life from nothing into whole. Breathlessly, I wait for you as you walked the other way, to turn around and come to me and tell me you will stay. Forevermore, please be with me, from darkness into dawn, as a mother deer holds tightly near to her newborn baby fawn. You will be that special one, till my life exceeds to live, and myself to you, I'll always live to give you all to give."* Lori, for all you have given me and everything we shared in life together, I thank you from the bottom of my heart. From the first day we met on the stairs leading down to your basement at your house on that cold winter's night in January of 1977, you asked me who I was, and then I asked you who you were, and we fell in love, and that's where it all started…

On a stairway.

To kneeling by your side, saying the Lord's Prayer to you, telling you it's ok, you can let go, and me telling you that I love you and will always love you, you gave me a little wink, and then I bent down to give you a kiss and with my hand on your chest as we kissed, that was the last time you took a breath and you died in my arms. My honey, my sweetheart, my wife; Lori, until we meet again in paradise, I will always love you, forevermore, your husband…Steve.

ABOUT THE AUTHOR

My name is Steven Zarycki. I was born December 16, 1961 in Paterson N.J. I was the oldest out of three brothers, had a normal childhood growing up, and my parents were of normal stature. I played baseball all my life as a pitcher; it was my passion. I was an average student in school, but at times my mind would be drifting off. I would be thinking about adventures that I never embarked on and focusing on what could be. I also couldn't sit still for a minute; I was what they called a *hyperactive child* and I never grew out of it. I had plenty of friends throughout my life; they taught me different things, both good and bad, and I, too, taught them things just the same. That was the whole part of growing up; to learn from your mistakes, to gain knowledge about right and wrong, and to succeed in life. But I never had a *best friend* that I could call or play with when I was younger. That is, until I moved to a town in northern New Jersey and fell in love at the age of fourteen with the girl next door. Her name was *Lori*.

Made in the USA
Middletown, DE
17 October 2015